D0064667

FROM BEHIND THE WALL

FROM BEHIND THE WALL

COMMENTARY ON
CRIME, PUNISHMENT,
RACE, AND THE
UNDERCLASS
BY A PRISON INMATE

MANSFIELD B. FRAZIER

Paragon House
New York, New York

First Edition, 1995

Published in the United States by

Paragon House
370 Lexington Avenue
New York, NY 10017

Copyright © 1995 by Mansfield B. Frazier

Library of Congress Cataloging-in-Publication Data
Frazier, Mansfield B.
From behind the wall : commentary on crime, punishment, race, and the underclass by a prison inmate / Mansfield B. Frazier. — 1st ed.
          p.   cm.
ISBN 1-55778-706-9
1. Crime—Sociological aspects—United States.   2. Crime prevention—United States.   3. Punishment—United States.
4. Racism—United States.   5. Marginality, Social—United States.
6. United States—Race relations.   I. Title.
HV6791.F73   1995
364.973—dc20   94-36317
                                                                          CIP

Manufactured in the United States of America

AUTHOR'S NOTE

While the words inmate, convict, and prisoner are somewhat synonymous in the public mind, to many of the incarcerated they can possess different connotations. In the text of this book I've tended to intermingle the three words; I, however, mean no disrespect to any of my fellow convicts anywhere by insinuating that they are inmates.

To Joel, who first believed . . .
and Donna, who believed soon after.

Duplicity, of course, is the basis of civilization.
—E. L. DOCTOROW

You've got to be honest to live outside the law.
—BOB DYLAN

*. . . and we intend to secure these rights . . .
by any means necessary!*
—MALCOLM X

CONTENTS

Part IV: Tragedies and Remedies 119

Part V: Politics, Media, and the Social Order 161

Part VI: Words and Admonitions for Black America 203

Acknowledgments

Many thanks to William Buckley, Thomas Flowers and Bob Mitchem. Without their gracious assistance with the English language no publisher would have bothered to look at the work. To Charles E. Rucker for his excellent proofreading (I think the "E" stands for "Eagle Eye"). To Chris Adkins and Vic Routt; they know what they did. To Lonnie Tolliver for providing me with the best of sounding boards. He greatly aided me in clarifying my ideas before committing them to paper. And to Penny Atwater, who proved to be a true friend when I sorely needed one.

PREFACE

Crime begins in the womb. When a disadvantaged teenager becomes pregnant and receives substandard prenatal care—which usually results in a low birth-weight baby—the cycle of a life which will eventually be spent, in some part, incarcerated has once again begun.

Medical experts know this child will encounter learning difficulties from the outset of his life. Couple this with the fact that the child will probably be born into a houschold where much value isn't placed on education, and, when time for preschool has arrived the mold is already firmly set.

The child will undoubtedly fall even further behind as he progresses through the primary grades, and before long will become a disruptive classroom influence to mask his feelings of failure and inadequacy. Some turn into bullies and challenge other children to join them in dropping out of the educational process, thus magnifying their own personal failure and perpetuating the low goals and expectations which plague our nation's inner cities.

By the onset of puberty, the child will begin to have his first brush with the law. If he lives in a neighborhood with gang activity, he will become a willing recruit and begin his life of crime in earnest.

These children graduate from juvenile crimes and courts to adult crimes and adult courts. Few manage to avoid some form of incarceration until they gain their majority.

The criminal-justice system is practiced in swallowing them up whole and eventually spitting them back out on the streets harder, tougher, and more callused to make room for the next generation of society's failures. At our present rate of incarceration by the year 2050, half of our nation will be employed watching the other half.

Many individuals in America, however, are satisfied with the status quo, at least as it applies to matters of race. They steadfastly refuse to draw a parallel between the oppressive conditions created by institutionalized racism and the rampant crime and violence we are experiencing. To make this admission would mean something should be done about those conditions if we seriously expect—and desire—to reduce crime. But there are some who would rather contend with soaring crime rates than admit to the racism which has created them.

Racism is as addicting as any opiate or alcohol, and over the years America has developed a huge habit for it. But, similar to the addict still in denial, nothing can be done about it until America is willing to admit the problem exists. Like the drinker who suffers blackouts and still maintains she has her problem under control, we tell the rest of the world we are not really that bad while more and more citizens die in the streets.

The problems of the underclass have been ignored for years. Even during the sixties when blacks were making huge gains in civil rights, the underclass remained largely unaffected and shut out of the process, prosperity, and progress. But similar to an infected and festering wound, the underclass continued to grow until it began to threaten the whole body politic. It grew mainly because it was, and by and large still is, ignored; and it's ignored because it is voiceless. This work is my attempt to give a voice to the voiceless underclass of America.

I neither need nor expect America to make an apology for how it has treated its black citizens for 300 years. No apology can undo the damage already done. What I—and every other citizen, black and of all other races—desperately need is for America at last to come to terms with the problems of the underclass before crime further destroys the fabric and quality of American life.

Every citizen, no matter what color, must be fully included in this experiment in democracy if we are to avoid igniting the powder keg of racism which is impatiently waiting to explode. We must not be lulled into a false belief that nothing is wrong by the periods of relative calm we experience. It would be far wiser for our leaders to take seriously the new cry of "No Justice, No Peace!"

A certain thematic redundancy runs through these commentaries out of necessity. I return to subjects a second, third, and in a few cases, fourth time to expand and clarify my thoughts and observations, and because I believe there are only a few basic causes for the racism blacks face in America. That racism underlies all of the poverty and crime found in poorer black communities. Although this racism wears many guises and is manifested in various aspects of American life in different ways, it is still the same racism blacks have faced since coming to these shores many years ago as slaves.

Before the Civil War there were no prisons in America for blacks, only for whites—slavery was prison enough. After the Emancipation Proclamation whites began using prisons, which had been in use in America only since the first half of the nineteenth century, as a means of "controlling" blacks. If sufficient laws didn't exist for this purpose, others were quickly enacted by panicked state legislatures during the Reconstruction. Little has changed legally since.

Certainly laws made specifically for blacks (and advertised as such) have long since disappeared, but only to be replaced by "selective enforcement" of existing laws to achieve the same result. There are some laws which blacks are crowding our nation's prisons for breaking that rarely get a white arrested.

The appeasement movement led by Booker T. Washington near the turn of the century had as one of its cornerstones the complete abandonment of blacks who ran afoul of the law by all other blacks. Blacks tactically agreed not to take up their cause no matter how trumped-up or unjust the charges against them. We wanted to prove to whites we were "good Negroes." To some degree, those feelings still exist in the black community. We fail to realize that as long as we allow any black citizen to be treated unfairly, all of us will continue to be treated in that manner.

Some blacks, as well as people of other races, have been so twisted by societal forces that they have adopted the violence done to them as children as a way of life as adults. These individuals have, by their actions, forfeited their right to live among free men. Society has a right and a duty to protect itself from those who would prey on it by violence. These individuals are lost to us. Nothing can be done for them.

We have to concentrate our efforts on insuring we don't continue to raise successive generations so mired in poverty, so devoid of hope, so beaten down before they've ever had a chance to rise up, that they become victims of, rather than credits to society.

Any failure of this work to accurately communicate the urgency and seriousness of the problems faced by the underclass should not be used as an excuse to say these problems don't exist or to ignore the message contained here, but should be realized for what it is: a failure on the part of the messenger.

March 30, 1994
Ashland, Kentucky

PART
I

THE CULTURE OF INCARCERATION

OUTLAW OR CRIMINAL?

THE COMMON UNDERSTANDING of the word *outlaw* makes it synonymous with *criminal*. But that is not necessarily true, or at least not the only meaning which can be ascribed to the word. Outlaw also can mean "one who lives outside the law."

Not above the law, not better than the law, just outside of it. One who realizes that the law—in his case and that of his race—is unfair and chooses to remove himself from its subjection; to as much as possible, ignore the law. But as Bob Dylan sang, "You've got to be honest to live outside the law"; when you reject the law of the land you must be prepared to replace it with something better, fairer, and more just.

I didn't set out to be a criminal. I had the same job for ten years; I was married (much too young at age seventeen) and had two children; I had two cars, a house in the suburbs, and a spotted dog named Peppy. But just when I was about to fully realize the American Dream it turned into a nightmare.

When I was rudely informed my future with my company would be limited because of the color of my skin, I was literally devastated. I firmly believed everyone was entitled to be treated fairly. I had pretty much lived a charmed life up to that point. This was the late sixties, and if racism indeed still existed it wouldn't last for long; the country was rapidly growing out of that sort of nonsense, I thought. When I was confronted with this beast on a personal level I was ill-prepared to handle it.

After a two-year struggle of trying to come to grips with my dilemma, I reasoned that if the game wasn't going to be played fairly, I would simply drop out. I would refuse to play the game. My marriage of ten years was in ruin due to my anger with racial bias; I couldn't tolerate going to the job I had formerly loved so much. I honestly felt I would do harm to someone. Besides, this was the sixties—everyone was dropping out.

I gave no thought to how I would earn a living without a job. My wife could well afford to care and provide for the kids since I'd put her through college and had left her fairly well set. But I was so blinded by the need to just get out I gave little thought to the matter of an income.

The era of filing civil-rights discrimination suits had yet to come to pass. Would I have taken that route if it had? I don't know. All I knew at the time was I had been invited to sit down at the table and play this game of life and I had played it by their rules. And had—even according to them—played it exceedingly well. Now they were saying I had been playing in a rigged game. The social contract didn't apply to me. They didn't have to honor the implied promise of advancement made to all who dedicate themselves to excelling.

Well, fuck it, I thought—if I'm to be treated unfairly then I'll live outside the law; as an outlaw.

After my savings ran out and the need to feed myself arose, I had absolutely no pangs of conscience about fooling society for my daily bread, the way I felt I had been fooled. One could easily say this is the mark of the true sociopath—someone who has no guilt. Others could say I am simply attempting to mitigate my guilt and responsibility for my actions by blaming the demon racism. It didn't deter me to observe that others of my race had come to this same fork in the road and hadn't taken the criminal path. My reaction at the time was simple: They were damn fools. Hit me, I'm going to hit you back, was my principle. That's why I didn't go south to march with Dr. King.

I adopted my own very strict code of ethics. I would never commit a crime against a person—I have never physically harmed anyone or taken anything from an individual. I've always specialized in swindling institutions, what I term "victimless" crime. The one time I almost killed a man (for snitching on me), fate intervened—for as God is my witness, I was going to kill him. Since I was not driven to a life of crime because of a lack of a means to earn a living, and since I had some skills acquired as a "square," I could afford to be somewhat selective about which crimes I committed. But those laws I chose to break I broke with gusto. Society had first breached the social contract with me, not I with society—all bets were off.

Had I not been educated incorrectly I would have had an alternative method of expressing my anger at society when it broke with me and vice-versa. I could have done something constructive with my rage, but at age twenty-seven when I turned out, I'd never heard of Marcus Garvey or

Carter Goodson, and was afraid of Brother Malcolm's message. I took the low, selfish road like a spoiled child.

The only regret I have is that I feel I have let my race down. I should have been in the forefront demanding change in the system that had so abused me; instead, I lived the life of a wastrel and libertine, and adopted the recalcitrant motto: "Living well is the best revenge."

I've come to realize I've never been a true criminal; I've never disrespected any law which respected me; I feel guilty jaywalking. Most of my race—like any other—would rather live in a society which is fair and allows men to be fair in turn. I've always, above all else, considered myself to be just that: a fair man.

However, it will take much effort, especially on the part of black Americans, to create a society in which all are treated fairly. We now live in a world where young black men see no alternative but to set out to become outlaws and turn into criminals. I pray for enough time left upon this earth at last to make my contribution to this worthwhile cause. I feel I deserve it.

GETTING TICKETED ON THE INFORMATION SUPERHIGHWAY

THE STERN-LOOKING JUDGE peered at me over the top of his cheaters. From his elevated seat on the bench, flanked on both sides by flags—one of the United States and the other bearing the seal of the Department of Justice—he looked exceedingly magisterial.

Well, there I stood again before the bar of justice. The charge: Violation of Title 18, Section 1029(a)(1)(2)(3) of the United States Code. I'd been down this road before.

I remembered the main rule: Never let them see you sweat. Bad form. After all, there are reputations to be protected here. In reality, there was no reason to sweat at this point; the deal had been done over two months prior. I had already pleaded guilty to manufacturing, possessing, and using counterfeit computer-access devices.

Since I was standing in a federal court in Cleveland, Ohio, rather than Los Angeles or New York, the judge was taking care to assure himself he completely understood the particulars of the case. My attorney had previously informed me this was the first prosecution ever in the Northern District of Ohio for actually making credit cards.

The judge's bailiff, a dour-looking black man about my age, gave me a withering look as if to say, "Why couldn't you just get caught selling dope like every other nigger who comes in here?" Most blacks who work for the courts look at the other blacks who come before those courts as if they are an embarrassment to the race. I look back at them as if they are the traitors, working for a system which incarcerates blacks at a rate six times that of whites for the same crimes—and for sentences 50 percent longer.

I had, however, proved to be somewhat of an embarrassment to some of the federal officials since the Secret Service agents had to call California for more information on how to properly charge me. I knew more about the laws governing my crime than they did.

I had received from the arresting agents a distinct feeling of extra consternation, as if to say how dare I, a black man, utilize purloined technology to cruise the information superhighway—something which has been in place for certain businesses for years—in what amounted to a stolen vehicle? They gave me a certain grudging respect, which only increased their consternation by the necessity of its being given.

The judge asked me why, since my jacket was getting pretty thick, did I persist in my chosen criminal profession. Didn't I realize that since this was my second federal case I was open for a twenty-five-year sentence? Certainly I did, but I also knew I wouldn't be receiving anything like that since I'd cooperated with the government. No, I didn't roll over on anyone. I'd turned in my counterfeiting equipment, which the Secret Service agents just loved getting their hands on, for an eight-month sentence for my woman and a three-and-a-half-year bid for myself. Plus a $135,000 fine.

Yes, my woman was down with me. I'm from the old school: If I'm going to throw bricks at the penitentiary, the least she can do is stack them up for me. I wince whenever I hear dudes who are supposed to be down by law brag about the good square job their wives or girlfriends have. Did Clyde let Bonnie work as a secretary or schoolmarm? I have to admit I'm partial to bad girls. As the saying goes: good girls go to heaven, bad girls go everywhere.

I thought for a moment before replying to the judge. I suddenly knew how Willie Sutton felt when he was asked why he robbed banks. For the money stupid. Always the money.

But that's not what I told the judge. Nor did I say what I now wish I had said: "Well, Your Honor, Neil Bush didn't call me to cut me in when he was raping the Silverado Bank out there in Colorado; neither Michael Milken nor Ivan Boeskey put me down on the junk-bond lick they were pulling off; my phone never rings in the middle of the night with an old school chum whispering the name of the stock he and his cohorts are going to manipulate on the market as soon as it opens in the morning. I guess I'm just underprivileged. You see, Your Honor, I never attended an

Ivy League school and received a master's in finance or a law degree so I don't have the same documents they possess. Milken only got two years. Bush didn't even get indicted. But I'm going to get three and a half years for . . . stealing without a license." Somehow I didn't feel too ashamed.

THE PRISON CONTRACT

A SIGN INSIDE the front door of the prison states, "Men are here as punishment, not for punishment." The punishment is for violating federal statutes; breaking the social contract. And while some may whine and moan, others learn to step off their time with as little hassle as possible—from other inmates or the staff.

The societal contract criminals break, however, is soon replaced by another similar one, based on prison rules, customs, and understandings. And this contract is just as enforceable as the one individuals in free society are expected to honor—enforceable upon prisoners and staff alike. You violate it at your own peril.

The federal prison system, similar to most state prison systems, has institutions of varying "custody" levels based on the seriousness of the crime committed and the projected length of sentence. They range from "supermax" institutions at the top end for lifers and those who still pose a threat even though incarcerated: mafia dons and drug-cartel kingpins. The new federal prison at Florence, Colorado, and Pelican Bay State Prison in California are examples of this type of institution. These are places where a convict's every move is scrutinized by a camera even though he is locked down twenty-four hours a day with his phone calls and mail closely monitored.

At the other end of the spectrum are the prison camps, similar to the one just outside the gate here at the F.C.I. in Ashland, Kentucky. In some camps inmates can wear personal clothing and the only sign of incarceration is a line painted on the ground which inmates are not supposed to cross. To many convicts these camps sound like heaven, but not to all convicts.

Many of the camps are run "chickenshit." For the privilege of having more liberty the inmates have to put up with stricter enforcement of petty rules by arrogant hacks, and with the constant threats of staff members to ship them off to higher-custody-level prisons.

At the "supermax" level there is no need for threats; the convicts have little opportunity to break any rules and there is no place left to ship them if they do. Their lives are completely regimented.

The next level down—maximum security—is a different story entirely. There men, although still controlled in their movement about the prison, have the opportunity to engage in the three most common rule violations: gambling, getting high, and sex. And the prison contract, to some degree, allows this type of behavior.

Regardless of how proponents of "lock them up and throw away the key" feel about it, a balance has to be struck between guards and prisoners which will allow the orderly running of an institution. If not, all hell would break loose on a regular basis while the arch-conservative is sitting safely at home watching football on television. The saying that "a liberal is a conservative who has been arrested and locked up" may be useful in solving the prison problem. These proponents of "tougher," more punitive prisons should rush right in to a max institution and show the experts how to do it.

The institution I'm currently at—a minimum-security joint—which is one step above a camp, has little sex, booze, drugs, or violence. There was a stabbing about six months ago but such violence is rare. Scattered drinking and marijuana smoking occur but they are not as much a part of the contract as they are in higher-security-level institutions. Guards constantly check for that type of activity here, whereas in a higher-level prison it is largely overlooked. If fact, at most medium and max prisons "drunk driving" won't even get you sent to the hole, as long as you don't cause any trouble and have sense enough to go into your cell and lie down when the guard gives you the eye.

The only infraction commonly "winked" at here is gambling. Card games and bookmaking on sporting events abound. It is not unknown for a guard to buy a ticket on a Superbowl pool from an inmate.

Occasionally, however, a guard (they are rotated every three months to keep them from getting too familiar with the inmates) who is bucking for a promotion and plans to make lieutenant by sending convicts to the hole for any and every little infraction he can catch is assigned to a housing unit. These guards are easy to spot: they never sit still in the guard's office; they constantly roam about, shaking down lockers; they are forever peering under mattresses hoping to discover something.

At the beginning of the quarter, when a new guard comes on, everyone expects to have his locker shaken down once or twice. The guard is just doing his job. If the guard spots an inmate or two who are always into something, be it arguing with other inmates, talking loud during the count, or running wild in the unit—a general "shit disturber"—then the guard may single these prisoners out for a little extra attention. Some inmates actually like to be leaned on by the guards; it makes them feel wanted and recognized.

But during one quarter we had a hero assigned to our unit. He made no distinction between the older convicts whom every staff member knows aren't into anything (or if they are they keep it quiet and aren't about to get caught) and the young wild dudes. At least this hack was nondiscriminatory—he messed with everybody, but as usual convicts had a way of messing back.

It started with someone smearing feces on the inside of the doorknob to his office. There was loud anonymous laughter behind his back when he discovered this little move. Next the fires began. Just small ones in a laundry cart at first, but they could get bigger. And the hack has no keys to the front door; he's locked up in there with us. Get the point?

Naturally the lieutenants and captain frown on setting fires. Since they can't discover who did it they usually will take one black, one Latino, and one white convict and lock them up for "investigation." After the next fire they take two of each, and then three. But the convicts know that before too long they are going to run out of room in the hole. Prisoners committing real rule infractions will have to make a reservation to get locked up.

And then one of the older convicts will slide up to one of the senior officers and lament the recent fires. The officer may be expecting the inmate to snitch someone out, but what he hears is that his officer is leaning too hard. Would he be so kind as to ask the jerk to back off a bit? The senior officer has to back his man up, everyone knows that, but usually within the week the officer is off to Siberia—patrolling the perimeter of the compound where he won't come into contact with any convicts. It's understood that the guards are allowed to maintain order because the prisoners let them. The prison social contract has been enforced; order has been restored.

A LITTLE SNIVELING

WITH THE AMOUNT OF CARPING and complaining one hears in federal prison on a daily basis, it would be easy to assume these places are snake pits. While many of my fellow prisoners would castigate me (if not something stronger) for writing this, they actually are not. Not that they are Camp Happy, either.

What they uniformly happen to be are fanatically clean, decent (if somewhat bland and monotonous) feeding warehouses for human beings. The fact that some individuals constantly complain has more to do with the fact that they are being deprived of their liberty than with the conditions they are living under. They would still complain if the place was a palace.

Which is not to say there aren't many daily aggravations, there are. While most of the rules, like them or not, are in place to insure the orderly running of a thousand-plus-men institution—and some fairly tough men at that—some of the rules are enforced in a petty and meanspirited manner. Usually it is not the rule itself, but which staff member is enforcing it. There is a saying in prison: "It ain't no fun when the rabbit got the shotgun." The staff controls both your movements and when you will eventually leave the institution.

The system functions on the principle of the staff ignoring any and every complaint they can, and then providing answers which are fuzzy, misleading, or downright mendacious when forced to reply. This code of behavior is enforced on every member of the staff (even those who might wish to provide a decent answer to a logical question) from the top down to the yahoos. No staff member wants to risk being called weak by another staff member.

One area where this attitude has proven harmful is within the medical unit. Since I've been incarcerated, there have been a few cases where prisoners were legitimately and seriously ill but their complaints went ignored or were taken lightly by the medical staff, who were afraid someone would pull something on them. True, there is probably a higher percentage of goldbrickers in prison than in the general populace, but other inmates shouldn't be allowed to suffer—and in one case die— because of them.

It behooves every convict to remain as healthy as he possibly can while in prison since the care and treatment are such that if a serious illness is contracted, the chances of having it properly treated are slim indeed.

One example of the pettiness is the recent changes in the procedure for something as simple as obtaining an aspirin. Formerly if an inmate needed aspirin, cold medication, antacid, or the like, he simply went to the pill line and received them. The inmate's number was merely recorded to make sure he didn't come back too often. The Bureau of Prisons—a multibillion-dollar agency—has recently begun selling these items to prisoners, at inflated prices.

In spite of these grievances, federal prisons perform their mission, which is housing law breakers in escape-proof, relatively safe environs fairly well. What they don't do, simply because it is not a priority, is to rehabilitate or train convicts in skills which are marketable in the real world. This, more than anything else, would reduce the recidivism rate. Sure, they have GED and vocational classes, such as welding, automotive mechanics, drafting, and a few others, but the fact of the matter is they are run like everything else is run: Do as little as possible for the convicts and see how many roadblocks can be constructed to prevent them from obtaining the training.

The problem is the system itself. It is designed not only to discourage inmates but often staff as well. Any organization which by design ignores the needs of one section will eventually ignore the needs of the other. Prison employees, by and large, are not a happy lot. The number of lawsuits filed by them against the Bureau of Prisons is much higher than in any other government agency.

A woman teacher I tutored for in a GED class is very close to burn-out. It happens a lot with teachers. Since she has dealt with the least-educated prisoners on the compound for the last twenty years, her frustration should come as no surprise to anyone. It would do her little good to complain to her superiors, since they, by unofficial bureau policy, won't do anything about it. A once-dedicated teacher is hanging on to her sanity by a bare thread and accomplishing little in the classroom. Other cases of the bureau basically devouring its own abound.

If the proposed prison "boot camps" ever come into existence and the government sees the wisdom and logic of instituting education classes for young first-time offenders, I hope they don't use the same people who currently run the prison-education system. My experience in prison tells me that they probably will; they always blame the failure of the program on the prisoners.

BACK TO THE BRIAR PATCH

LIBERTY IS a very subjective concept. One man's prison is another man's palace.

On a scale of one to ten, with ten being the death of a spouse or loved one, going to jail or prison ranks about an eight for most folks. Prison, it is popularly held, is not a place anyone would care to go. Stories of beatings, killings, and rape—as well as other deprivations—spread by sensationalized accounts in film and other media, firmly establish them as living hellholes.

At the opposite end of the spectrum, cries are heard from the "moral" right, who falsely accuse prison officials of turning institutions into "country clubs" which do nothing but coddle criminals. While both extremes are equally wrong in their perception of prison life, most people wouldn't care to find out the truth of the matter first hand.

There is a saying in prison that applies to a certain percentage of inmates who, by virtue of their addiction to alcohol, drugs, and other self-destructive behavior, "weren't arrested; they were rescued." In many cases, the saying is deadly accurate.

Generally speaking, it is only the older convict who can readily admit he feels more secure, comfortable, and at home in a prison setting than he does on the street. But even though most younger convicts won't admit it, many of them feel exactly the same way. It is called "becoming institutionalized"; to adapt so well to the rules and routine of prison that life on the outside becomes the aberration, prison the norm. Some just can't cope with the fast-paced world and its temptations and function better in an environment where they are protected from themselves.

A mid-level-prison staff member, a fairly intelligent man with some degree of compassion, once remarked to me that if he, upon becoming aged and infirmed, had no family to turn to he would rather throw a brick through a post-office window (good for a five-year federal sentence) and wait for the police to arrest him, rather than go to an old-folks home. The fact that prisoners tend to venerate older convicts, and little of the abuse that occurs in nursing homes occurs in prisons (at least to older inmates), seems to support his logic.

Many people of the underclass grow up in grinding poverty, and lack the basic securities about tomorrow most of us take for granted: that there will be food in the cupboard; that someone (who is not drunk or stoned out of their head) will be there to provide stability; and that they can go to sleep and awaken with a reasonable expectation of remaining free from harm. These people come to view incarceration as a respite from a world in which they have no control. At least in prison they know what the next day will bring.

After their initial incarceration, during which most of their fears concerning their ability to handle prison life are allayed, people of the underclass soon learn the rules they are expected to abide by—and which ones they can get away with breaking—and otherwise settle in to step off their time. Free from the everyday fears they faced on the street—becoming victims of violence and having to struggle, often without an education, to make ends meet—they find a home like none they've ever before known. The second time around, it's like throwing Brer' Rabbit back into the briar patch.

While I don't like to personalize my writing, my case is somewhat similar to those individuals who are "rescued." I had—or knew how to get through criminal means—enough money to live comfortably anywhere in the world. I also had a secure childhood which allowed me to function in society with ease. What I lacked was the discipline to do what I wanted to do more than anything else—write. I had attempted on numerous occasions over the last ten years to gain the self-control necessary to cloister myself and learn the craft I wanted to pursue, but to no avail. Something, whether it was a call from a crime partner with a new moneymaking scheme or a championship fight in Las Vegas, always managed to distract me. Of course, the problem was me. Now, however, free of those distractions, I am forced to confront my shortcomings and have been provided with the near-perfect setting for writing, albeit without a decent research library. I hope that upon my release I will be able to maintain my focus and continue with my craft, but that is yet to be seen.

However, I am surrounded by men, both young and old, who will never again be able (if they ever were) to function in free society. They are products of a racist system which is still cranking out youth, both black and white, who due to their environment—will one day become a burden on society. One of the yardsticks Amnesty International uses in determining the rate of human-rights abuses in a given country is the percentage of population incarcerated. America leads the world in this category; yet, our government can find good cause to point the finger every place else. To many members of the underclass—myself included—prison has become little more than a rite of passage.

JAILBIRDS OF DIFFERENT FEATHERS

THERE ARE TWO TYPES of inmates I find somewhat amusing. One is the political conservative. For years, he advocated a "lock them up and throw the key away" mentality toward those who run afoul of the law, but now that he has become ensnared in the criminal-justice system he is left bewildered. You can almost see him wanting to cry out, "Hey, I'm one of you guys! I've voted straight Republican for years, how can you do this to me?!"

While the prison administration does acknowledge these inmates as former pillars of the community, at least in terms of giving them better jobs and living accommodations, the clock still moves for them at the same rate it does for every other inmate.

The problem these convicts have is they steadfastly refuse to see themselves as guilty. They may have pleaded guilty in court to the indictment, but once in prison they revert to a mindset of total innocence. This allows them to view themselves as different—and better—than their fellow inmates. And if they do admit any culpability, they earnestly feel they should be treated better than the common criminals they are forced to live among, like the young man who, after killing both his parents, threw himself on the mercy of the court because he was now an orphan.

These souls live in a netherworld; they don't fit in with the other convicts, but can't get too chummy with the staff. Even when two of these former staunch allies of the status quo get together, they offer each other little comfort, since each has the attitude, "I know *I'm* not supposed to be here, but I'm not so sure about you."

They view their crimes as "exercises of privilege" rather than violations of the law. In their eyes, crimes are things the lower classes commit, not solidly middle-class defenders of the American Way like themselves.

I sometimes wonder what these guys' lives will be like once their sentences are completed. Will they be ostracized by their former friends and business associates, or will they be welcomed back into the community with open arms? I would assume, knowing the attitudes of most citizens (who view themselves as above and beyond getting caught committing crimes) that these ex-convicts will be about as welcome as lepers. Not so much because they broke the law, but because they committed the sin of being apprehended.

The views they held before their arrests will come back to haunt them upon their release. These men, who still cling to their conservative beliefs (albeit somewhat changed in light of their prison experiences), are likely to remain social pariahs for the rest of their lives. And while I know it's meanspirited for me to feel this way, somehow this thought is very comforting. Sort of just desserts for those who were so narrow-minded and who lacked self-knowledge so profoundly before their fall.

The other inmate who evokes laughter is the jailhouse lawyer. He becomes an expert on all of the laws, rules, and regulations of the court system, as well as of the prison which houses him. He spends his time tilting at the windmills of bureaucratic procedure.

While some of these "lawyers" become fairly knowledgeable about certain narrow aspects of the law, to most of them it is not the right or wrong, win or lose of any given situation, but merely the argument itself. They just love to squabble. What they are failing to realize (or maybe they do and just can't help themselves) is the fact that there is only one place where they can "get their thing off," and that is in prison. There exists no comparative situation in free society. If someone carried these confrontational attitudes to the workplace, he would soon be fired.

Those who become addicted to fighting the system and the staff soon become bored upon release. They quickly long for the environment where they feel they have some degree of control, or at least where they are being listened to. If nothing else, when an inmate complains in writing (no matter how ridiculous the incident or situation about which he is complaining) his existence is acknowledged, a validation he may be hard pressed to find on the street. He can only return to prison to "play the game."

There are many ways to do time. Some pump iron, many gamble on cards or sports. I choose to write. Maybe I shouldn't be too hard on those convicts who choose to do their time by fighting the system. Indeed, if some of these convicts didn't rebel in this manner their days would be miserable. Having a gripe to wake up to in the morning may be the only thing that keeps them waking up.

However, this attitude just doesn't play well on the street. Most of these inmates have to be imprisoned to be happy.

THE FIRST

IT CAME FROM OUT OF THE BLUE; totally unexpected. I hadn't been at work five minutes when my foreman, an affable old-timer who had started out as a guard and had worked his way up to an administrator in the furniture factory I work in, told me someone from my housing unit had just called. I was to have my belongings together and be in R&D (receiving and discharge) by 9 o'clock.

My sphincter muscle tightened.

Since I definitely wasn't scheduled for release, at least not for another fifteen months, it could only mean one thing: I was going back to court to get another sentence—more time.

The county immediately south of Cleveland, Summit, had filed a detainer against me five months prior. The detainer is a legal document that states a jurisdiction has charges pending against a convict, directing the prison officials to "detain" said convict until they send a couple of deputy sheriffs to pick the convict up and return him to the jurisdiction to face the music—once again.

I had known about the detainer since it had arrived at the institution. I had, in response, filed an interstate waiver form, (commonly known as a speedy trial waiver), which gave Summit County 180 days to complete the process of coming for me and getting me into court. Years ago, a jurisdiction holding an indictment would wait for a convict already in prison to finish one sentence, then pick him up at the gate and take him back to try, usually convict, and sentence him on the next case. It was generally agreed this was a tad unfair, ergo, the Interstate Agreement on Detainers had been made the law of the land.

The additional sentence I was facing (I was going to plead guilty since I had no chance of beating the case) wasn't much; the charge wasn't at all serious. I would in all probability be able to get it run concurrent with the one I was currently serving by pleading guilty, which meant I would still have the same release date I currently had. The only problem was it would require me to sit in a funky county jail for two to four months to complete the process, and I'd had enough bad food, being around fruits and nuts, and interruptions to my writing for one bid,* thank you.

My first thought was of my writing. What of my work hadn't I sent out of the institution yet for safekeeping? Would I have time to mail some other work out before I was trussed up in chains like Mad Dog Earl for the trip back to Ohio?

The thing was, I had managed to make my situation as comfortable as possible, considering I was in prison, in the last thirteen months. I had a job which allowed me to get personal typing in and a decent cell—in short, I was jailing pretty well. I knew it would take some doing and time to get things back in order after my return. Damn! And my writing was going so well!

It wasn't like it was completely unexpected—I had been hoping that they would just let the time limit expire. It was a bullshit charge and many jurisdictions simply don't have the resources to waste on picking up prisoners already serving time to give them sentences which won't affect their release date. I had been sneaking up on the bulletin board in my unit every day after work hoping my name wasn't on it for transfer back to Ohio. Damn, damn, damn! And I had skated for 150 of the 180 days! Oh, well.

Even though it had been a blow, I had taken it like a real convict. None of the other four or five inmates who had heard the foreman drop the hammer on me saw me sweat. Then as I returned to my desk to put some paperwork in order in preparation for my imminent departure, the foreman gleefully cackled "April Fool's!"

My bladder damn near betrayed me. The foreman had had no way of knowing about my outstanding legal difficulties with Summit County. It was just one of his standard April Fool's jokes: Report to R&D. Only afterward did my hands begin to tremble.

Throughout the rest of the morning, I set them up and he knocked them down. When one of the guys would come into the area, I would tell them the foreman wanted to see them in his office. This was always said very solemnly. Since this wasn't in itself too unusual, the guy would blithely walk in. I would stand outside the office and watch through the window as he told them to "report to the lieutenant's office." Dreaded words to any convict. There was never good cause to have to "report to the lieutenant's

* Blacks say "bid"; whites say "bit." The judge just says "do it!"

office"—it meant your ass was in some kind of trouble. Guys that walked into the lieutenant's office normally walked out in handcuffs, headed to the hole.

The foreman and I could see the guy's mind working. What had he done that someone could have snitched on him about? In prison, virtually every convict has committed some infraction—usually on a weekly, or even daily, basis. Most of them don't rate going to the hole, only receiving warning or a "shot" (an incident report). The worse thing that would result was extra duty, such as mopping a floor or washing walls. Twenty hours tops, but clever convicts don't like to even get these. Number one, it said you were a cluck, and number two, (and much more importantly) you'd just given the staff something to use to deny you certain privileges toward the end of your sentence, such as going to a halfway house for six months. The more shots you receive, the less halfway-house time.

The first guy we got was a tough Italian out of Chicago named Rovy. He took it like a stand-up guy. We could see his mind working but nothing else. As he put on his coat and walked out of the office I asked him in a conspiratorial voice, "What's up?" "I don't know," he answered sotto voce. "Keep your fingers crossed I make it back." Going to the lieutenant's office was indeed like going on a mission. Most didn't return.

As Rovy headed out of the main door the grinning foreman stuck his head out of his office and again yelled, "April Fool's!" Rovy broke into a big grin as we dissolved in laughter. "You motherfuckers," he muttered as he walked back to his work area.

The final guy we got didn't fare so well. He was a younger convict. When the foreman dropped it on him his knees buckled. He quickly recovered, but they'd buckled nonetheless. Mercifully, the foreman didn't let him sweat too long before letting him off the hook. That final guy had made our day.

Prison had just made the young convict a lot stronger.

THE WRONG CHICKEN LINE

PRISONS ARE THE MOST segregated institutions in America. While I may work with whites and men of other races at my job as a quality-assurance clerk in a furniture factory, and while the cell to my left houses two Latinos, and the cell to my right houses two whites—all of whom I'm cordial with if I speak to them at all—I eat and sleep only with other blacks.

No white or Latino will be assigned to bunk with me (unless the institution is on full and there are absolutely no other beds available, and then only for a few nights to a week at most) and the two lines in the chow hall remain distinctly self-divided along racial lines. Whites and white-skinned Latinos upon entering the chow hall go to the right; blacks, darker-complected Latinos, Native Americans, and the few Asians go to the left. And never the twain shall meet. One of the main causes of the 1993 riot in the Lucasville, Ohio, prison was forced integration in sleeping accommodations.

During the sixties and seventies—the period of my callow youth—I would have found something disturbingly wrong with this situation. No bigger booster than I for the newly emerging American order of integration could be found. My wife and I were true believers in the school of thought which held that full integration would lead to equal opportunity for all and it resided right around the corner, a corner which America was about to turn. We put our money where our faith was and purchased a home in a "planned integrated community." Seven years after we moved in, the much-heralded community was virtually all black. It takes two races to integrate.

Today America remains nearly as segregated as it was before the flurry of civil-rights activity of the sixties. While many blacks now live in better circumstances, they are basically still living segregated, albeit in upscale enclaves. But we tried back then—oh, how we tried. And we suffered the deep disappointment known only to true believers.

Maybe age and experience bring with them a creeping cynicism. Then again it just may be wisdom. Whichever the case, I now accept the fact that America will remain, despite the odd exception, a segregated society. Will blacks' chances for full opportunity be damaged by this? Certainly. But I feel we have little choice but to again pursue "separate but equal."

To select "separate but equal" over continued pursuit of unsuccessful integration is not giving up on our rights to full, equal participation in American society—it is simply the wiser, more attainable course of action. We can't keep spinning our wheels pursuing something which isn't going to happen. The former may be difficult to achieve but the latter is impossible.

In reality, integration is only a method of attempting to guarantee equality. Counter to what many whites feel, blacks are not dying to live next door to them. We just realized they were going to reserve the best schools and city services for themselves, and we demand the same level of public service. The only way we could insure this was to move next door. If "separate but equal" can actually be achieved, everyone would be much happier. In prison, I live the proof of that statement everyday.

No one here is unhappy with the virtually complete separation of the races. In the unit, the white guys get together and play poker and the black guys play spades. Sometimes the gamblers, black and white, play poker together for money without incident. Occasionally, an interracial game of eight ball is observed in the rec room, but not too often. The writers' group I belong to is integrated, as are education classes, though blacks and whites sit on different sides of the room. But the truth is, everyone is happy because everything is equal. Straight down the line. And if it isn't, someone is going to holler.

A new black convict who worked in the kitchen taking the food to the serving line decided on his own to give his homeboys the favored chicken breasts on the black serving line, and the less desirable thighs on the white line. None of the whites said a word when they saw what was going on. They simply all got into the black line until the attending staff member corrected the situation, which didn't take long. I can assure you, the blacks would have done the same thing had the situation been reversed.

A small minority of people of both races live above the color line. I pride myself on being one of those. I don't give two hoots what color you are—your actions and opinions are all that matter to me. However, those of us who feel that way are in the minority. For most Americans, it just won't work.

The problem with America is that blacks have been getting in the white line. They have no choice if they want equality. And they will continue to create disturbances by getting into the white line until we have true "separate but equal."

DOING THE TIME

I DON'T TRUST A MAN who doesn't wear a watch. He doesn't know what time it is. And time, even here in prison, is important. Time is unremitting, unforgiving. It is the one thing no one can ever get back—Shirley Mac-Laine aside.

Some men in prison prefer to do their time completely unaware of the clock or calendar. They attempt to forget the year, as if ignoring time will somehow make it cease to pass or stand still for them while they are doing time. But of course, it doesn't, for nothing can stop time from making its inexorable march into the future.

We should ally ourselves with that which is inevitable; we should make time our friend rather than view it as an enemy. Gain from time rather than simply allow time to slip past without providing us any benefit. For that which we don't benefit from infallibly harms us in some way. Nothing important is neutral.

Some people attempt to play games with time, as if they can outsmart it. They are frustrated by their lack of ability to control time so they contrive methods to cheat it. They challenge the clock in various ways.

They fail to rise early enough in the morning to prepare for the day, or if they do they dally about, seeing how close they can cut it before being late for work. They like to arrive exactly on time, with no time to spare. In this way they feel they are in control of time. They begrudge every minute they arrive early. But time remains completely unconcerned. All of their efforts to beat the clock are futile. Time, in the end, always wins.

People who watch the clock to arrive without a second to spare have already lost, even if they arrive exactly at the time they planned. Time has made them hew to its keeper, the clock. And when you are late—as inevitably you will be—time extracts the price of throwing the rest of your day off. You can't beat time.

The only game I play with time is in concert with it. Upon awaking, I immediately look at my watch to check the time. My goal—or target time—is exactly 6:00 A.M. Every morning I note how closely I awaken to my target time and try to reduce the amount of my deviance from it. Currently I am down to plus or minus thirty-five seconds. Some would say this is a silly prison game or that I have become a slave to time. Not so. I view it as being in closer harmony with time. The more I am master of the clock, the more I am master of myself in other areas. Time, you see, is my friend.

It wasn't always thus. For years I was out of harmony with time. I wanted to develop whatever talents I may possess as a writer but I couldn't "find the time." As if time were hiding from me or was lost. Time of course wasn't the problem—it was me. I didn't know how to utilize time; I was undisciplined. Doing time has changed all that.

If I hadn't been forced to do time I would probably still be out of sync with time. My way of utilizing time before was to rush around as fast as possible trying to "save time" to have "more time" to do the next thing as fast as possible so as to "save still more time"—time to do the next thing as fast as possible. . . . But I still never seemed to have "enough time."

Faced at last with the prospect faced by all prison inmates of losing precious time, I at last began to learn to use time lest it simply slip away. I certainly can't get back the years I have spent in prison, no more than anyone can retrieve yesterday. But at last the secret of time dawned on me: It is *how* the time we have allotted to us is spent. Nothing more, nothing less. Today. Right now. This split second.

Once I learned that, I found I have the time to do more things than ever. Although I am incarcerated, I work a full-time job (though I do spend a good portion of my time at my typewriter working on my own projects— my good friend time allows me to do this) and still manage to turn out a respectable quantity of what I hope is credible work. My prison sentence could be summed up this way: "It was the best of times, it was the worst of times." I now use time wisely and therefore have all of it I need. In fact, I have enough time to last me the rest of my life.

TRYING TO KEEP ABREAST

TWO DISTINCTLY DIFFERENT schools of thought exist about how convicts should deal with the outside world. One can be capsulized by the jailhouse rhyme, "Keep you mind off the street and your hands off your meat." The other view, which I personally adhere to, is to remain as involved as possible with the outside world, while still following as closely as humanly possible the dictum expressed in the last part of the rhyme.

Not that I hound the telephone trying to keep in close contact with Baby and what she is doing—it ain't that kind of party. It's not that I don't care, it's just that she's out there and I'm in here. I don't care what she had for dinner last night, nor do I wish to tell her about the swill I had.

Some convicts facing "Buck Rogers Time"—a parole date which is so far into the next century (2010, 2020) that they can't even imagine getting out—avoid what's going on in the world for their own sanity. Time, for them, is standing still. One guy who has served twenty-three years joked to me, "I heard they've got airplanes out there."

I'm somewhat lucky. I don't have a ton of time to do, and I live in a housing unit with enough other mature inmates to insure that one of the two television sets in the unit beams in a cable news program every morning from 6:00 A.M. until at least 7:30 A.M. I'm often there for the three repeats of the half-hour broadcasts. Evening specials are a bit more difficult to get scheduled. Sports and action movies dominate the screen then. But if the program is of singular significance we sometimes do gang up and force the airheads to either watch and become informed or leave the TV room. Many choose to exit.

However, some choose to stay. About once a month or so a new dude who has bad county-jail manners will check into our little hotel. Often two of these jerks will come into the TV room together. You know the type, beetle-browed Neanderthals with knuckles dragging the ground. On the street they can be found in movie houses talking back loudly to the screen, purposely attempting to ruin the film for anyone else. Rarely are you able to see who these bird brains are in a darkened theater, but just as you might have imagined, they're brutes with IQs lower than their ages, punks just waiting for someone to tell them to shut up so they can go off.

But this is prison, and they *can* get faded in here.

What usually happens is that one of the old-timers (like me) will simply go to the television and turn the volume up. If they talk louder, I turn it up again. They can't—no matter how loud they talk—out-volume the television. Some of them will glare at me; I glare right back. If they say something (which rarely happens) they'll get the standard lecture—in front of everyone in the TV room—about convicts learning to respect each other. If they take a dim view of my words of wisdom, they can do something about it.

No doubt one of these young gangbangers would make instant mincemeat out of my old ass. I know that, they know that. But then they'll have to have eyes in the back of their heads because they'll never know when I'll be coming up behind them with a shank. And I will be coming, on that they can bet. However, the fact that I will take up for myself means I'm respected and don't have to.

Before things get to that point, someone will have summoned Bubba. I helped pull a legal thorn out of Bubba's foot (got an old charge dismissed) and he's been extremely grateful ever since. And Bubba is a great guy to have in your debt—when he walks on the yard he blocks out the sun. At six-foot-eight and over 400 pounds, all Bubba has to do is walk into the TV room and ask in that booming voice of his, "Are you all right, Mr. Frazier? Nobody fuckin' with you or anything, right?" I look at my *former* antagonists and smile. "No Bubba, nobody's fuckin' with me." Bubba lumbers off back to his cell where he draws the most delicate, heartwarming greeting cards you can imagine.

It's not too surprising that many of the younger convicts would rather watch MTV than C-Span, but when Congress is debating a crime bill which could have a direct effect on their freedom (one issue under consideration is a sentence reduction for first-time offenders) you would think they would be interested, but no. They would rather ask me later what was said and how it affects them than give up their rap or hip-hop for an hour or so.

On Saturday mornings when no one has to go to work, a few of them will arise around 9 A.M. with nothing to do. While awaiting the 10 A.M.

weekend breakfast call, they'll drift into the television room, drawn by the sound of talking heads. Belonging to a generation addicted to watching anything that moves on the screen, they stand transfixed, mouths agape, staring.

In another few moments what I call the Saturday Morning Debating Society is in full swing. Invariably a news story they can relate to—one about crime, punishment, or drugs—is flashed on the screen and they're off to the races. Before long, five or six of them are yelling and screaming at the top of their lungs attempting to make their point. I can hear them even though they're in a supposedly soundproof television room and I am in my room with the door closed some thirty feet away.

This morning's "debate" concerns whether blacks, fed up with racism, can take over the country. Some argue it could be done; others argue it can't, they would all be killed. One of those who takes the pro position firmly believes it can be done since there are more blacks in the country than whites anyway. Ah, the limits of being raised in a ghetto.

The argument rages on. Their belief is that whoever argues the loudest and longest is the rightist. It sounds like World War III is about to jump off. My people sure can be loud!

In fact, the only other time I've heard such screaming and yelling was once when I visited the floor of the New York Stock Exchange. Young white men were bellowing away . . . for money. Well, at least my young black brothers are screaming out for justice.

My other sources of information are the newspapers and magazines carried in the reading library. Some convicts, usually older ones, read their way through a bid. When I'm not writing (or shooting pool for my limit of fifteen hours a week), I read. While the library is somewhat limited by the publications the prison subscribes to, there are a dozen or so of us who share the publications we personally subscribe to. Although my budgetary constraints keep a few of my favorite publications off my list, I do manage to stay abreast of current events.

Another source of information is an excellent National Public Radio station which broadcasts out of Ohio University, located in nearby Athens, Ohio. In a sea of country and western, top-40 miasma, and stations which seem to do nothing but give hog prices (remember, I'm doing my time about twenty miles on the southern side of the Cotton Curtain), it has been a welcome beacon of intelligence indeed.

Classical music during the day and jazz in the evenings, interspersed with news stories on everything from the fight to save the whales to a piece on a Chinese blues singer. I certainly owe this station, which depends on public donations, a contribution when I get out of here.

The local studio hosts on NPR—I refrain from calling them mere disk jockeys—are young, bright, and talented. On Sunday mornings, they have a program of folk music I love to listen to which goes by the curious name of "Below the Salt." They play lots of Bob Dylan. It is a peaceful accompaniment to my Sunday-morning prayers, the time I set aside to assure my own God in my own way that I remain in complete submission unto His authority, and am thankful for His revealing to me the things He would have me to know. Ruth Brown, one of my favorite blues singers growing up, hosts a blues program later on in the evening. I manage to lose myself in the music and conversation, and, for a few hours, escape an environment made cruel by monotony, ignorance, and despair. The mixture of music featured on Sunday—zydeco, bluegrass, jazz, and folk—reminds me of the overriding sameness of mankind: We all love music, and a smile is a smile in any language or culture. My hope is that one day all of us—no matter what our backgrounds, ethnicity, or differences—can live in harmony and that peace will reign.

Then I have to return to reality.

MY FRIEND BILLY

I GUESS IN RETROSPECT I should have seen it coming; any fool would have. Not that I would have changed anything if I had. No, I definitely wouldn't have changed anything, and in fact, I won't even now, after the fact.

It had to do with Billy, the Mad Bomber. Billy's doing forty years for making and selling bombs. He doesn't talk about his case much (few guys doing a load of time do) but from what I can gather one of the bombs he sold, which was supposed to be used to scare someone in a business deal gone sour, wasn't properly placed and some people were injured. But that's beside the fact.

For, in addition to his more nefarious activities, Billy also managed to obtain a master's degree in English on the street. He's a heck of a writer, and he is currently working on a long piece about the history of Native Americans of the Great Plains, a subject on which he is an expert.

Much of whatever I've learned about writing in the last fifteen months I owe, at least in part, to Billy. Once he saw that I was serious about my craft he was more than willing to help me master the fundamentals I had glossed over in high school. Reading some of my first efforts now I realize how truly atrocious my writing was.

Billy, however, proved to be a very patient instructor, albeit a ruthless editor with little use for sloppy thinking or writing. He encouraged me when I became bogged down and was (and is) supportive as the rejection slips from publishers mounted ever higher and higher. "It's all in the game," Billy said philosophically.

In short, Billy has been a true friend.

Did I mention Billy is white? Well, that's probably because I don't view that fact as very germane to our friendship, or anything else for that matter. But, as I will relate to you dear reader, not every convict here is of that liberal bent of mind.

A few weeks ago I got another new cellmate. J.P. was a well-educated, fairly well-to-do hustler from Atlanta. He is also a militant black, and to my mind, a racist.

Upon arriving at the institution (he'd done plenty of time before and was prison slick) he surrounded himself with a cadre of younger convicts who quickly became sycophants. Since J.P. once studied law and many of these young men have trouble even reading, he used his knowledge to his advantage when they came to him for legal advice. He enjoyed being the hog with the big nuts.

While some jailhouse lawyers look at the facts of a case and give an honest appraisal of what they can or can't do, J.P. never read a case he couldn't win a reversal on. His camp followers disintegrated into a group of whiners who spent 24-7 grousing about how rotten the government is. What else is new?

J.P., a master manipulator, used derision and ridicule to achieve domination in situations where his knowledge of the law failed to give him the upper hand.

As my cellmate, J.P. was privy to my personal habits. I like to snack on apples, cheese spread, and peanuts. J.P. expressed the opinion that this was "the strangest shit I've ever seen!" I laughed it off the first time. When he made the same comment a few days later, as if to say, "how dare you have the nerve to eat this again after I've passed judgement on it," I backed him off. "It's an acquired taste," I said, laughingly. "*I* acquired the taste for it, *you* didn't. If it bothers you, then don't watch me eat it."

The next day after Billy had dropped a magazine off to me, J.P. asked what was I doing "kickin' it" with a white man. "Here comes trouble," I thought at the time. Not satisfied to personally live by his twisted code of prejudice by himself, he was going to attempt to force me to live by it, too. I wasn't too surprised, since I had long before realized this type of convict inhabited the compound and came in all shades. But I'd never had to cell with one before.

"J.P.," I responded, "sometimes you talk like a man with a paper asshole." Thinking back, it was probably the most imprecise imprecation I've ever hurled at anyone, but that was the best I could do on short notice. It, however, served the purpose.

Two days later the unit gossip gleefully told me that J.P. was spreading the rumor that I wanted to be white. The next day the version I heard was that I *thought* I was white. I wondered when one stating I *was* white would surface.

I needed this shit like I needed a hole in my head, but no one—*no one*—was going to dictate to me who my friends were going to be. J.P. and I would soon have to lock ass.

Never mind that I'd been in the unit for over a year and got along pretty well with most of the convicts who wanted to get along. I, in fact, had done minor legal work for about a third of the prisoners in the unit, mainly the young blacks among whom J.P. was spreading his rumor. I often performed this gratis, since sometimes they arrived at the institution with no money and less hope. But according to prison rules, if I didn't do something to stop J.P., what he said must be true.

The unit was buzzing. Men who go from day to day without a thought of tomorrow eagerly looked forward to the fight they knew was sure to jump off. I would have to check J.P. for "getting off in my business" or suffer the consequences. Their anticipation was palpable.

Fate, however, intervened the same evening I was going to confront him. J.P. got into a shouting match with the easiest-going hack on the compound—a guard who hadn't sent anyone to the hole in the five years he'd been working at the institution—and J.P. was sent to the hole. *Whew!* It wasn't that I was afraid to fight J.P., it was just—like I said, who needs this shit?

While in the hole, he threatened another officer and was shipped out to a higher-level hellhole of a prison, about seventy-five miles away, on a disciplinary transfer.

When things had gotten back to normal, Billy, who must have heard about what was going down, finally broached the subject. We laughed about the smallmindedness of some convicts and then he told me the nickname he'd acquired among a few of the white inmates due to our friendship: nigger lover.

INMATE EDUCATION

WHEN NO LESS RESPECTED an elected official than Senator Arlen Spector (R-PA), a member of the Senate Judiciary Committee, calls for rethinking the manner in which we attempt to rehabilitate first- and second-time offenders, the country has to take notice.

Senator Spector, a fairly conservative Republican and former prosecutor, writing in the *New York Times* (January 4, 1994) is one of the first, and few, politicians with courage enough to speak the truth on this volatile issue. Only his impeccable conservative credentials will prevent the position he takes from being labeled heresy by orthodox ideologues of the right.

Senator Spector rightly states that providing convicted felons with marketable skills during their period of incarceration isn't coddling them; it is simply the best way to insure that they never again have to prey on society because of a lack of a marketable skill by which they can gain employment.

While his no-nonsense approach (which I fully concur with) leaves room for life sentences for those criminals who are beyond rehabilitation, basic realism compels him to state we simply cannot lock up everyone for life who commits a crime. Eventually we would produce a society where half the citizens are guarding the other half.

Historically, rehabilitative efforts have left much to be desired, especially in terms of reducing recidivism rates.* Many criminologists now believe programs designed to turn law breakers into law-abiding citizens

---

* Recidivism figures are always bantered about, put to whatever use politicians can devise for them. When the public hears that somewhere between 60 and 80 percent of felons return to prison, it is assumed that a released bank robber goes out and robs another bank or a mugger mugs another citizen. While this is sometimes the case, actions like these are in the vast minority. Most inmates return to prison on a parole violation—usually for "dirty urine." A parolee can smoke one marijuana cigarette and be sent back to prison for it, and his "violation" is counted as "new criminal behavior."

just can't work. Based on the percentage of ex-felons who return to prison, I can readily understand how they have come to their conclusions. I am not a big believer in the desire of a certain percentage of inmates, in certain age brackets, to mend their ways upon release. Success can better be achieved with the younger or older prisoners.

A large portion of my lack of faith in rehabilitative efforts, however, is due to do the wrongheaded methods and systems employed to carry out the programs as it has to do with the prisoners themselves. Most of the prison education programs just aren't taken seriously by prison staffs.

This is understandable since prisons' first mission is to keep people safely locked away from society. This is done very well, but it takes a different mindset to educate prisoners, and most penal experts just don't have that mindset. I know I've written on this subject previously, but it's so vital an area it bears repeating: Programs in which the administrators have no confidence can't and won't work. And most prison staffs have little faith in prisoner education. The staffs in charge of the programs sub-consciously *have* to engineer the failure of the programs to validate their point of view and methods of controlling prison life.

Not too long ago, educators became aware of the need for culturally relevant education for minority students. They found this approach had much improved success rates. Maybe the same principle applies to pris-oners. Programs designed for their specific needs, taking into account their shortcomings and limited world views, would no doubt prove more suc-cessful than current techniques, especially at the beginning of the education process. And if they were administered by people who had faith in them.

Incentives have to be established, since most prison inmates are prone to "immediate gratification syndrome." They have trouble making the con-nection between doing well in school now for a payoff in the future. To formulate programs that take these different variables into account isn't coddling, it's just an effective method of education. But one that won't be successfully carried out by prison educators in the present system.

How long will we continue to allow the game to go on whereby programs which have little chance of success are allowed to be put into motion simply so some racist can, upon their inevitable failure, say, "See, I told you it wouldn't work"? And of course the failure will be charged off to the convicts. Who else?

We need to provide these men with marketable skills with which to make an honest living. If they then choose to return to a life of crime only then should we lock them away. For good.

THE JOKE IS ON SOCIETY

IS CRIME PREVENTION really just a joke in America? Judging from a vote by the U.S. Senate it must be. Our senators love to take to the floor of the Senate and thunder about crime and what they are doing about it for the safety of the public, but when they had a chance to make a real difference they were found wanting. They voted to curtail Pell Grant payments for prisoners.*

The grants, named after Senator Claiborne Pell, are given to help defray the cost of higher education in America. Since prisoners have no income, all of them who possess a high-school diploma or equivalency qualify for the grants, which amount to a maximum of $1,500 per year for each inmate/student who goes to college all year. Many don't attend classes all year.

Senator Kay Bailey Hutchinson, in an opinion article in the March 17, 1994, edition of *USA Today*, argued against providing the funds for prisoner education and stated prisoner Pell Grants cost the government $200 million in 1993. In a companion article, which argues for continuance of the program, Senator Pell stated 27,771 prisoners in state and federal prisons received the grants in 1993—less than 1 percent of total prisoners.

27,771 times $1,500 (even though all of the student/inmates didn't receive the full amount) comes to only $41,656,500., which is quite a bit less than the $200 million figure Senator Hutchinson touted. It is still

* Two days after Congress voted to eliminate Pell Grants for prisoner education during the 1994 Crime Bill debate, they voted to require inmates to pass the high-school-equivalency exam or lose the standard fifty-four days a year "good time" which is deducted from every inmate's sentence. It seems our political leaders want prisoners to obtain an education—but not too much. Maybe just enough to continue failing. Another example of that supposedly august body sending mixed and confusing signals based solely on political expediency.

an impressive sum—until you consider what America is receiving for the money.

Senator Pell accurately stated that 97 percent of all inmates will one day be returning to society. The national recidivism rate is somewhere between 60 and 80 percent. That means roughly 600,000 to 800,000 of the million men and women who will be released from prison sooner or later will again commit crimes. However, only 10 percent of inmates who receive two or more years of college while incarcerated will commit another crime upon their release. How then could the Senate vote to cut off the Pell Grants, which provides for most of the education?

Senator Hutchinson disingenuously argued that allowing convicts to participate in the Pell Grant program takes funds away from needy and deserving children, maybe even the children of police officers (note whose children she cites. This is demagoguery at its best, folks). However, Senator Pell, who sponsored the program and therefore should be more informed about its workings, stated it "functions as a quasi-entitlement: A student qualifies for a grant and the size of the grant depends on the availability of appropriations." No qualified student can be denied. Both the convict and the cop's child would get a grant—if the cop didn't make too much money, which is usually the case.

Senator Hutchinson complained that some of the funds go to shady operators who specialize in running schools which are in existence only to show inmates how to milk the Pell Grant program while providing little in the way of real education. If this is the case, why doesn't the government do something about the slick operators who are taking advantage of both the inmates/students *and* the government? The prisoners don't have access to the funds themselves; a staff member has to sign off on the applications and cut and send the checks. If these schools are ripping the government off, put the operators in prison where they belong. Or would putting a stop to these shady operators offend her Republican sense of freewheeling enterprise? After all, they are businessmen. Instead, she would rather throw the baby out with the bathwater.

I've tutored GED classes. The need for convict education is very real. I would prefer to see paroles granted on the basis of a convict acquiring a marketable skill. Mandatory education is required for any child under the age of sixteen. Why? Because anyone who doesn't have an education will soon become a burden on society. But since our educational system is failing at an ever-increasing rate, we have hundreds of thousands of young people in the country with no job skills. Many of them eventually wind up in prison. Once these youths have gotten themselves into prison we should do the job we failed to do before—educate them before releasing them. Whether they like it or not.

I guarantee you the classes would be well attended. Or is crime prevention really just a joke in America?

HIDDEN COSTS OF INCARCERATION

"POWER CORRUPTS; absolute power corrupts absolutely." While the staffs of prisons don't have absolute power, the amount of it they do have is just enough to corrupt some of them.

The majority of the guards and other staff view their authority as just part of the job; something they have to have to maintain order in a tough environment. But there are others who, never having had any real power of their own before, let it go to their heads. Convicts quickly learn who these petty tyrants and mental midgets are and how to avoid them as much as possible. The joke, in the end, however, is on these sick individuals who become drunk on power. They soon take their twisted attitudes home with them at the end of the day and inflict them on their families. Once they allowed themselves to be corrupted by the intoxicant of control over someone else's life without the experience or moral maturity to deal with this power, eventually it negatively affects them and their long-suffering families more than it ever does the convicts. One proof of my theory is the extremely high divorce rate among prison staff, which is even higher than that of police officers.

No doubt prison officials attempt to hire the best possible people they can for the various institution jobs. But while some children want to grow up to be firemen and policemen, I don't recall (and I doubt if you can either) any of my playmates wanting to grow up to be prison guards.

It should also be taken into account that working in a system which, by its very nature, turns a deaf ear to complaints as a method of operation, will eventually subject those who run the system to the same disregard.

Those in charge of the system, if they are going to maintain an air of toughness, must pay almost as little heed to staff complaints and problems as they do to complaints lodged by the inmates. By the time most of the new staff members discover this aspect of the incarceration environment, they have already been optioned by the benefits of working in such a system.

Since most prisons are located in rural or semirural areas, the individuals hired for the job are generally not too sophisticated, too educated, or too ambitious. The majority of them view their positions with a steady employer as a sinecure, and wouldn't leave them to go to heaven. And staff expansion is their surest route to fast promotions.

Those citizens and elected officials who constantly call for harsher and harsher sentences for social, economic, and medical crimes should be required to spend their weekends acting as prison guards. For rarely are the problems indigenous to guarding prisoners considered by those calling for draconian sentences. They neither know of nor care about the effect of spending one's life in a prison setting. They have as little real regard for the keeper as they have for the kept.

Prisons are necessary in every society. Law and order couldn't be maintained without them. But there are those who excuse our soaring prison population rate—the highest in the world and fastest growing—with the notion that it is the necessary by-product and function of the freedoms we enjoy as a nation. This is pure myth. Other countries which enjoy similar freedoms don't have near the number of citizens in prisons as America has. Politicians and voters take note: the victims of our failure to adequately deal with crime are not only those who suffer at the hands of criminals, but also the people who are charged with guarding those convicted of crimes.

Not in *My* Backyard!

PRISON IS a true societal microcosm, magnified and distilled by the proximity of its convicts. Whatever opinions, attitudes, and prejudices individuals harbor while at liberty are brought with them to incarceration. Little wonder prisons are self-segregating, racist institutions; they are only mirror-imaging society at large. The juxtaposition of men who in the free world would assiduously avoid each other if at all possible makes for strange, and sometimes violent, interactions.

The milder phenomenon of incarceration is invisibility. Convicts of different races, backgrounds, and cultures often look "through" each other, denying the other's existence. Disconcerting to the new prisoner at first, but at least not violent.

In higher-security institutions—or those "gladiator schools" that house a preponderance of young hotheads and gangbangers—violence is all too commonplace. The convicts segregate themselves into ever-reducing sub-groupings with homogeneousness being based not only on skin color, but even on what section of a city one originates from. Not content with black against white, or Latino against whoever, they succumb to low forms of tribalism peculiar to prisons.

Everyone has to "ride" with someone for self-preservation. God help the loner convict caught not "in the car" if some shit jumps off. His ass is out.

And prison officials just love it. These self-defeating attitudes are condoned, encouraged, and in some cases outright fostered by prison administrators. Their biggest fear is that the convicts will one day wake up, stop viewing each other as the enemy, and turn their collective pent-up frustrations and hostilities on them, the staff.

The staff, who are drawn from the surrounding rural communities, often have had little or no contact with cultures other than their own. Sensitivity

43

training is rarely given to prison guards; in the few cases where classes are held, the training has little impact on their xenophobia. They view their mission as simply one of warehousing human beings. Little or no thought is given to the fact that 97 percent of all prison inmates will one day return to society.

One current bit of monumental stupidity in vogue in the black community is the efforts to rebuff state and federal officials who attempt to build prisons in rundown black neighborhoods. I'm not talking about stable, tree-lined black neighborhoods; these are weed-choked fields and urban areas with boarded-up buildings. Yet black city councilmen rise up in righteous indignation and rail against the building of these institutions in a sad parody of white suburbanites. As if there were some property values *left* to protect in these depressed locales.

They would rather send their own sons, daughters, brothers, mothers, and fathers to some backwoods corner of the state where visiting is difficult and the treatment of the prisoners bad. The rural whites actively solicit for prisons to be built in their areas since they know the steady paychecks from the institution will stabilize their economies, just as they would in the black communities if the leaders had an ounce of common sense. It's not like modern prisons are sardine cans where convicts will be leaving on a regular basis, roaming the neighborhood, killing the residents in their sleep!

Rather than keep our family members close to home where we can help heal the wounds inflicted by racist courts, we pretend we have "vested interests" to protect! We should be protecting the members of our race as best we can. We should be deeply ashamed of ourselves for our heartlessness and gross stupidity.

America is not yet ready to end its mindless orgy of incarceration. It will continue to attempt to enforce unenforceable drug laws and use prisons to hide the living, breathing failures of our social system away from the vision of the world. For the foreseeable future, prison construction will continue to rise at a rapid pace as the by-products of institutionalized racism are converted via "three strikes and you're out" legislation into lifetime inmates.

America has painted itself into a corner. In order to continue justifying the large number of blacks imprisoned due to selective enforcement of laws, the system is incarcerating larger numbers of middle-class whites, something it never intended to do. In this way, racism is now visibly impacting on whites as well as blacks, but then it always has.

The root cause of the latest round of laws and crime bills (which do nothing to reduce crime) results in politicians' willingness to lock up anyone, just to look tough on crime and gain reelection. As such, shouldn't convicts begin to view themselves as political prisoners? They certainly are, at the least, political playthings.

If the young convicts, who currently take out their anger and frustration on each other with stabbings, beatings, and killings, could be made to understand how a system which created—and then failed—too many have-nots is responsible for them being where they are, then maybe they could be convinced that the way out of their present purgatory is through education and enlightenment, not maiming and killing.

I WISH

EVERY ONCE IN A GREAT WHILE I sit around with other convicts and play "I wish." It's a form of daydreaming particular to individuals who live continually in a state of deprivation. Being separated from past lives of luxury, or, in some cases, making plans to live large in the future, the words of Shakespeare were never truer: "Nothing is, but what is not."

It can be a very illuminating game. Men reveal themselves by what they wish for. For instance, a friend of mine, a Latino dude who is still fairly wealthy (even after forfeiting millions to the feds) wished for a dump truck full of cocaine. He is currently in prison because he was knocked with a thousand-kilo shipment of the devil's dandruff.

His wish sort of amazed me; he'd rarely used drugs on the street. Since we were all just wishing, I wondered to myself why he didn't wish for money, like I did, or maybe health or long life. The only reason he could have wanted a truck load of cocaine was to sell it. For money. Why not just wish for the cash instead and avoid all of the heat?

Carlos wished for the drugs because drug dealing had come to delineate who he is. It's his persona. It has little to do with the money; he has money. It's all about the power. He's as addicted to selling drugs as some people are to using them.

Carlos is from Miami and still owns a small chain of men's-clothing stores which family members run. His parents are fairly wealthy also. He got into drug dealing because it was "glamorous." In a culture which worships the memory of Jesse James and John Dillinger, he began to see himself as the newest cult hero: the drug-dealing outlaw.

At the beginning of his career there was a woman involved. Isn't there always? But this particular woman had him enthralled. He could get lots of women, but he had to have Maria.

Carlos was doing well. He had the clothing stores, a piece of a newly

46

thriving retail computer business, and drove a $200,000 sports car. He had his Cigarette moored at the yacht club. He was learning to pilot a small aircraft. But Maria wanted to be a gunmoll. She was raised in a neighborhood where drug dealers were the dudes to look up to. She wanted the glamour of being associated with bad guys, but rich bad guys.

They both tooted a little cocaine every now and then—all of their friends did. But Maria knew someone who knew someone who could get this great deal on some kilos. When Carlos balked at the idea she calmly stated that if he didn't have the heart for it she knew someone else who did. After she stayed away for a week and refused to return his calls, Carlos cornered her at a nightclub and pressed her for the drug hookup.

In her world—which was soon to become his world—money was simply money, but drugs were power. The pecking order is established by how many kilos you're moving a week. With Carlos's business acumen he quickly rose to the top of the heap.

When Carlos was in the big time, his every wish was someone's command. He didn't have to slip around to see other women, Maria brought them to him. This was a high-rollers privilege, and Maria was proud to have a man who deserved this kind of treatment. She loved to show him off to other women. She also knew that by selecting the women they partied with she could better maintain control over his appetite for them. Carlos was in cocaine heaven.

But the drug changes people. At first, Carlos had said he would just do a couple of deals to make Maria happy. But just as Maria knew would happen, he got hooked on the lifestyle. The aphrodisiac of power, on being "The Man."

He now had henchmen with Mac-10's. If he wanted someone smoked all he had to do was say the word. Of course there were other men who could speak on him in the same manner, so alliances had to be formed, truces brokered. He became a nation in miniature unto himself. And then someone did something stupid; someone always does. He got caught dirty and he rolled over. Carlos was set up by the DEA with the aid of the snitch. It was a dead-bang case. They made sure they did everything by the book for once, no loose ends, no illegal searches, no doctored testimony. Carlos caught thirty years. Buck Rogers Time. His parole date isn't until the year 2015. Naturally, his mouthpiece told him he would get the case reversed on appeal—lawyers always say that. If Carlos thought paying $300,000 for thirty years was a bad deal, the additional $150,000 he paid for his losing appeal must have seemed much worse.

Of course, Maria is long gone. She hooked up with another drug dealer right after Carlos lost his appeal. Carlos looks for the new boyfriend to show up here one day or another. The bitch is bad luck, he figures.

So for now, and for the foreseeable future, (2015 is just too far away to imagine) Carlos sits here with me and 1,200 other souls, thinks about the good times he used to have, the cars and boats he used to drive, and plays "I wish."

PART
II

RACISM AND ITS WAGES

Racism Is Here to Stay

GIVEN THE FACT that blacks have been in America for more than 400 years, emancipated for more than 130, and have yet to achieve full equality, it is not illogical to conclude the "melting pot" theory simply cannot work in our case. As disheartening as this presumed fact might at first seem, for blacks to continue to labor under any other assumption—and worse, to conduct the affairs of the race based on such assumptions—is dangerous and foolhardy.

Much of the despair, poverty, and crime found in our nation's ghettos can, and should, be viewed as the by-product of the economic war which has been waged on our race. While we can now go, eat, and sleep wherever we please many of our race cannot take full advantage of these rights due to the continued financially disadvantaged condition racism keeps them in. Full financial equality will prove to be the hardest hurdle for us to overcome in our fight for full equality.

The "can do" spirit of our nation—the resolve to meet any challenge head on and beat it—makes the fact that we can't seem to solve the problem of institutionalized racism all the harder to accept. The fact that matters of fairness and justice are involved (matters our nation takes great and undue pride in being world leaders in) only makes it that much more difficult to admit that this national disease will remain uncured. How do you solve a problem you won't admit you have?

Blacks have to learn to live, and live comfortably, with racism. To fail to do so will continue to cause us great harm. For if we fail to acknowledge this fact of American culture, and the permanence of it, we will continue to become victims of the bitterness and rancor which has, in the past, prevented us from reaching our goals. Racism is damaging enough without our shooting ourselves in the foot by allowing it to make us bitter, too.

This should in no way be construed to mean we should passively accept racism, institutionalized or otherwise. Blacks, as well as well-meaning whites, should continue to press for its complete elimination from American life. As a nation, we just can no longer afford it. But too many blacks are letting the struggle get to them. They are so upset over racism it becomes debilitating—in other words, just what racists want. We have to engineer our lives in the manner that best negates the effects of racism. We musn't let it pull us down.

In the foreseeable future, no black will be elected president. In that regard, the American Dream, of which this is a cornerstone, remains forfeit for us. No black, no matter how well qualified, will work his or her way to the head of a Fortune 500 company before this century's out. The negative effect of middle-class blacks bumping their heads on the glass ceiling of corporate culture is already apparent. These blacks, who should be reaching back to help their less fortunate brothers, are becoming disenchanted with their prospects in white corporate America. They aren't mentally preparing themselves to help the next generation of upwardly mobile young blacks following them into the corporate world, let alone less fortunate blacks.

The ideal of every American advancing on nothing but merit is still too great and cherished a dream ever to completely to be given up on. But for blacks to make career decisions based on a yet-to-be-fulfilled dream is less than prudent. It would appear wise for these blacks to look to owning their own businesses in the black community, where they can employ other blacks, as their ultimate salvation. I know this is easier said than done, but if we're going to work hard it should at least be for ourselves.

Maybe young blacks, immediately after college, should seek employment in white corporate America for a number of years to help advance the cause of racial equality, but not make plans to commit their lives to that employment structure. The chances of their eventually becoming frustrated are simply far too great. After learning all they can they should then seek to use their talents in their own communities among their own people.

To admit much of the racism we currently encounter is beyond our abilities to rectify is not admitting we condone or will forever accept it. It is simply a matter of finally taking the wiser course of financial independence as our means of combatting it. Once our race is less dependent on a racist system for virtually everything—including our basic happiness—we will fare far better. And thus economically armed, we will be able more surely and swiftly to surmount the walls of institutionalized racism.

A "Just" Man's Place

In RECENT HISTORY, Buddhist monks in Vietnam immolated themselves to protest their oppression; in England jailed members of the IRA continued their defiant hunger strikes until death; and in America members of the Black Panther Party were branded outlaws and criminals by the government, hunted down, imprisoned, and killed.

Since the government has taken legitimate protest against racist oppression and branded it criminal behavior, it is little wonder that currently the only form of serious black protest comes under the guise of criminal activity or rap music. And some wish to ban rap.

Does anyone seriously believe that if the promises of fairness and full equality that were made to blacks during the fifties and sixties were actually implemented we would be experiencing the levels of violence and crime now occurring in the black communities throughout the land? Leaderless rebellions which lack clear direction always degenerate into mindless criminal activity and violence, but the root cause of this violence remains racism. The feeling among many urban black youths is, "So what if we burn down our own neighborhoods? They were nothing but slums anyway. We've got to live somewhere, so we'll just gradually move into your neighborhoods and burn them down, too."

"Under a government which imprisons any unjustly, the true place for a just man is also in prison," testifies Henry David Thoreau, writing in *On the Duty of Civil Disobedience*. I will use this bit of wisdom in an attempt to bring the terrible killing going on in the black community into some sort of perspective. This rending of the social fabric of the country unfortunately seems to many the only means members of the underclass have to draw attention to their plight. Without headlines decrying seemingly senseless murders they and their problems would be completely ignored. If this is the price we must pay to rouse America's conscience, then so be it.

It is now abundantly clear that white America has no intention of doing anything meaningful to ameliorate the wretched conditions of the black underclass until it runs out of other options of maintaining peace and order. Its back has to somehow be placed against the wall before it will act. Once the prison population soars high enough, social change will occur. Hence, young blacks are filling our nation's prisons with alacrity and pride.

I feel ashamed, saddened, and dehumanized that I personally have been so buffeted, twisted, and turned by incessant racism that I sometimes have to stop myself from gloating when I hear or read reports of whites being afraid to walk the streets at night due to rampant crime. They are victims of the same terror I often feel. They surely understand that it is their race's prejudiced attitude which has created the charged atmosphere of violence they are so afraid of. Don't they? In voices trembling with rage, young blacks ask by their actions, "Why should you whites be allowed to go about your business unmolested while we suffer so?"

Terms like urban-survival syndrome and cultural psychosis are becoming part of the lexicon as sociologists and defense lawyers attempt to explain the driving forces behind the violent headlines. Similar to the plagues in the book of Exodus, where Yahweh turned the water to blood, sent locusts to destroy crops, and struck down every Egyptian first born, America will continue to suffer the pestilence of violence until the yoke of oppression is lifted off the black race.

In this professed "Christian" nation the question I have to ask is not when this lifting will occur—for occur it eventually must—but why the moral errors of our society, and what has to be done to correct them, aren't abundantly evident to everyone: politicians, clergy, civic leaders, and average citizens.

"A minority is powerless while it conforms to the majority; it is not even a minority then; but it is irresistible when it clogs by its whole weight," wrote Thoreau. If our "clogging" of this corrupt, racist system has to take the form of filling prisons with black bodies as fast as they are built until the country is taken to the brink of bankruptcy, then again, so be it. Enacting spurious laws designed to lock away the "race problem" will not end the plague; only the fulfilling of the guarantees promised to all Americans in the Constitution will.

"Let every man make known what kind of government would command his respect, and that will be one step towards obtaining it." The violence in our black ghettos is the voice of a voiceless people screaming an enraged *no* and a defiant *never* to a political system which says by its deeds that blacks must forever accept their present condition and hope to live only severely limited lives.

"A majority are permitted, and for a long period continue, to rule, not because they are the most likely to be right, nor because this seems fairest to the minority, but because they are physically strongest." Other societies have had to learn the hard lesson taught by the sniper and bomber. This black wreaking of havoc on society is *exactly the same* as that which Thoreau discussed—and the same as the organized, political resistances in other countries of the world. Eventually it will have the same effect—causing change.

"It is not desirable to cultivate a respect for the law, so much as for the right. The only obligation which I have a right to assume, is to do at any time what I think is right." America expects blacks to respect laws which do not respect them. This is not going to happen. That angry young blacks have not had their grievances articulated in a manifesto which white social scientists can consume and ponder doesn't render those grievances any less legitimate.

America has the most ruthless mechanisms for dealing with unwanted dissent, made all the more effective because of its insidiousness as it wraps itself in the mantle of righteousness.

The calls by whites for blacks to control the unruly and violent elements within the black community often fall on deaf ears simply because these young blacks are acting out of the frustrations felt by blacks who are too timid to perform these acts themselves. But rest assured, as soon as the white majority makes serious attempts to raise the jackboot of oppression off of our collective black necks, the black community will respond by causing the violence to cease.

I abhor violence with a passion second only to the passion with which I abhor oppression. Even a fool would rather address grievances with the olive branch of peace than the fiery sword of violence—and we are not fools. But our minority status in America enables us to respond to oppression with the sole means available to us: the sacrifice of young black lives.

THE BLACK CHILD IN A STRANGE LAND

HISTORY AND LITERATURE are both replete with individuals who being denied the opportunity to become heroes instead become villains. Often these individuals have physical afflictions which make them so grotesque that their chances of a normal existence, let alone stardom, fame, or even normal success in some field of endeavor, are severely limited. Others not so afflicted by foul chance are held back from great achievement only by what goes on in their own heads. Environment can have severely limiting effects.

But whatever the cause of an individual's limitations he often still aspires to noteworthiness, and if he can't be president or pope he often becomes determined to be the antithesis of good. He discovers fame and infamy are but two sides of the same coin of the realm, and may come to the conclusion that if he can't rule in heaven, he'll serve in hell.

A somewhat similar process is occurring in our nation's ghettos. Part of the American Dream is that any youngster, no matter how humbly born, can aspire to one day be president. While we know the need for presidents isn't large enough to accommodate everyone's desire (regardless of what the multitude of political aspirants for the position might think) the mere holding out of the possibility of such a lofty achievement to our nation's youth is part of what molds them into responsible citizens. Maybe not presidents all, but contributing citizens nonetheless. Just having the dream is beneficial.

But what of the children who learn early on in life they must lower their aspirations? That, well, you see, ah, the country just isn't quite ready for a minority president yet. Where is their portion of the American Dream?

"Well," the child might reason, "I'll just become very rich instead. I'll be the head of a large corporation!" Er, ah, well, no—your chances (no matter how hard you study and work) aren't very good there either.

Often children of the ghetto aren't told what they can be, only what they can't, and the list is fairly long. In other cases, parents, reluctant to tell a precocious child the heartbreaking reality that racism limits her options in life, let the youngster continue to believe her future is as unlimited as anyone else's. No one wants to be the one to tell a child our society is so designed that she, no matter how bright, isn't eligible for the grand prize. I can't blame them. I wouldn't want to have to tell my child about this invidious fact of American culture either.

However, no matter how onerous the task, our children must be told of the realities of the racism they will face and how crippling it might be to their career and life options. To neglect to tell them borders on the criminal. Yes, they must be told, and told in a manner which lessens the effects of this racism on them as much as possible. The earlier a black child knows the accurate, unvarnished history of his race and what to expect from a society mired in institutionalized racism, the better his chances will be to counteract these negative forces. One of the root causes of disenchantment on the part of black adults is not being informed of the realities of American life as children. And no matter how bitter racism has made the parents, they should teach their child about racism in a way in which that bitterness isn't transmitted.

To make a child bitter about his limited prospects only insures further limitation. No doubt the child will soon enough have negative experiences on his own about which to be bitter.

Blacks in America are, and shall forever remain, strangers in a strange land. The melting pot hasn't worked for us because it can't. However, this doesn't mean we can't be happy and successful here, or should necessarily contemplate emigration to Africa. On the contrary, once we fully realize the accurate facts of our continuing existence in America and make positive moves to take the future of our race into our own hands, we'll find we can coexist, prosper, and be content in a basically hostile environment.

We have to begin raising a new generation of black youths who not only realize the facts of our economic position but are educationally, psychologically, and emotionally prepared to meet the challenges of racism— and triumph. Never mind that some might call training of our children in this manner overly Afrocentric. The cold hard reality is that unless we properly prepare them, we're at risk of losing a large percentage of our race to the effects of racism in the forms of incarceration, drug abuse, alcoholism, and early violent death.

We have to convince our youth that they can succeed in a racist climate; they can prosper in spite of grossly unfair economic conditions; they can be the forerunners of a new generation of black men and women who finally carve out a place for us at the table of economic justice in this indeed "strange land."

OUR DEAR OLD SICK UNCLE

BLACK AMERICANS, in spite of the treatment we've received at the hands of a basically racist system of government, remain amazingly loyal citizens. We know our Uncle Sam is a deceitful old bigot but he is the only uncle we've known and we love him in spite of his faults. People have an innate need to be proud and feel part of the country which they are citizens of and blacks are no exceptions. Boxing promoter Don King's bombastic posturing aside, his "God Bless America" campaign of a few years back was, without a doubt, very sincere and genuine.

But the foregoing doesn't mean we don't realize our dear old uncle is seriously sick. That he definitely is. His mind is addled. Not only does he treat his black nephews and nieces shamefully, he also treats gays and lesbians, Native Americans, and other minorities who lovingly call him uncle disrespectfully, too.

He has, out of ignorance and greed, allowed havoc to be wreaked on the environment—pollution of the waters, clear cutting of the forests, strip mining of the land, and the dumping of toxic wastes. He often ignores the very experts he hires when what they tell him conflicts with special-interest groups greedy for a fast buck at the expense of future generations. He can be a cantankerous and stubborn old coot.

However, when we criticize him, it is in the way of concerned relatives who care deeply for a still-respected family patriarch. The world is changing around him though, and he is going to have to give up some of his antiquated views and prejudices if he is going to keep apace. Gone (or going) are the days when he could simply flex his military muscles and get his way. The new world order is going to be based on economic rather than military might. If he continues to run around the world criticizing others about how they run their houses while doing nothing about human-rights violations in his own home, he is going to start looking like a doddering old idiot. Some are already snickering behind his back, and if it wasn't for the fact he is so wealthy they would be laughing in his face. Since the world is gaining economic equality, it won't be long before someone embarrasses him, if indeed he is capable of being embarrassed.

We blacks, browns, reds, and gays who loudly call for Uncle Sam to change realize how old folks can become set in their ways. Old habits die hard. But the cancer of racism, the cirrhosis of sexism, the clogged arteries of gay bashing, and the tuberculosis of toxic waste is killing him. Our cries for change are cries to save his life. We want to make him well, well for all of his citizens. He is in critical condition and no one wants to break the news to him.

We blacks even threatened to run away from home, so disgusted we've become with the treatment we receive. When we at last became familiar with the country of our origin we became fascinated. It was like discovering a long-lost mother. Oh, we knew where Africa was. But you see, we had been taught to fear her. She seemed so strange to us. The only things we knew about her we'd learned via Hollywood. She ate her young, we were told. She was very poor and unruly. We'd even been told she didn't want us; that we weren't welcome there.

When we finally discovered the truth we were elated. We became intrigued with her rich history, vibrant colors, and wonderful sounds. We began to dress in the clothes of our forbearers and sing the songs of our ancestors. If our uncle didn't want us at least our mother did.

She gave us a sense of who we were and where we'd come from. Something we'd been lacking for centuries. She gave us a much-needed past. A sense of identity; something every group needs to prosper. She gave us something to be proud of.

Now many of us choose to live straddling two cultures. We live in the home of our uncle where we were born, but in which we, in many ways, still remain strangers. But we increasingly identify with the home of our mother Africa. Rather than divide us internally, this dual identification has only served to make us stronger. It has made us the complete people only someone with a history and heritage can be. It has made us more assured than we, too, deserve to be accorded full and equal treatment in our uncle's house.

We may go visit our mother Africa. We may even stay for a while. But we'll always be coming back to our uncle's house—our home. For that's what America is to us: home. We, too, are Americans.

THE BODY COUNT

My FRIEND BILL just walked out of my cell scared, depressed, and confused. He'd recently gotten off the phone with his seventeen-year-old son who had given him the holiday body count.

Out of his son's group of four young black friends, all from relatively good suburban homes, one (the nephew of a world-famous boxing promoter) was in police custody for killing another youth, shooting him thirteen times, and another was in hiding from the police for another shooting incident in which the victim also died.

Bill's son swears he wasn't involved in either incident, but since the shooters in both cases were such good friends of his son, Bill is naturally very concerned.

Of course, our conversation eventually turned to what is wrong with the black youth of today. We listed all the usual suspects: the breakdown of the family; the ready availability of guns; the preponderance of violence on television; the dearth of jobs for black teenagers, and so on. We didn't spend too much time on the subject of what to do to curtail or reverse the present trend.

The largely symbolic Brady Bill comes too late for these youth, both the victims and the triggermen. Any gun-control measure will be too little too late for thousands of other youth, both black and white. For once I agree with the National Rifle Association; we can no more control gun violence (at least in the next ten years) by controlling the buying and selling of guns than we can control drug use by attempting to control and regulate drugs. This is not to say the gun laws shouldn't be tightened, they should. But we should be prepared for gun prices to skyrocket without any appreciable reduction in gun violence. We must also be prepared to come to terms with the soon-to-flourish black market in weapons. There are simply too many of them around.

The problem in the black community has reached critical mass. We are under serious threat of losing a large percentage of the youth of our race to violent death if something isn't done, and done quickly.

In years gone by, juvenile judges threatened the occasional wild youth who came before them with incarceration or an option: to join the military. It was a reasonable alternative to jailing them and in most cases it worked. Many a young man who was forced into the military in the fifties and sixties found himself, via the imposed discipline, changed for the better.

Now, however, a young person without a high-school diploma or with a criminal arrest need not apply to any branch of the military. This option for youth cutting the apron strings no longer exists. And when it comes down to it, cutting the apron strings is what it's all about. As society changed and the military option disappeared, we failed to realize what we were losing or make any attempts to replace it. Now these youths remain in the community, or briefly go to juvenile facilities where they only enhance their criminal knowledge and behavior, and are soon infecting other kids. The problem now grows exponentially.

Now that our neglect is coming home to roost with murder and mayhem, we must be willing to bite the bullet and do what is necessary. The boot-camp/prison idea for young first-time offenders is a good start, provided we compel the youth use their time there constructively.

Sentences should be for an indeterminate period of time, based on how soon the youths complete high school and learn a marketable skill. If they accomplish this in two years, fine; if it takes them ten, so be it.

We have to be mentally prepared for some of the youths who never gain a skill that will make them employable. A certain percentage will refuse to get with the program, simply because they don't want to leave the institution and return to society. I know this may be hard for the average citizen to comprehend, but this is a fact of life in the underclass. How many times will these youths be pushed back out the doors of the institutions when they don't want to go, only to have them commit another crime in short order so they can quickly return? Better to allow them this face-saving method of remaining where they are than for society to provide them with more victims as a reason for their return.

Naturally, well-meaning protectors of the Constitution and Bill of Rights will howl long and hard if the type of program I'm suggesting is implemented. Under other, more normal circumstances, I would be howling right along with them. But circumstances aren't normal in our nation's ghettos and the piecemeal approaches we're currently using just aren't working. I understand that certain groups want to protect the rights of these youths, but as the situation now stands the only right these youths have is the right to die young. We have a duty to protect these children from themselves.

SECTION 1091: "GENOCIDE"

"GENOCIDE" IS THE heading of Title 18, Section 1091 of the United States Code. The law book states:

(a) BASIC OFFENSE—Whoever, whether in time of peace or in time of war, within the boundaries of the United States, with specific intent to destroy, in whole or in **SUBSTANTIAL** [all emphases added by author] part, a national, ethnic, racial, or religious group as such,

1. Kills members of the group;
2. Causes serious bodily injury to members of that group;
3. Causes the permanent impairment of the mental facilities of members of the group through drugs, torture, or similar tendencies;
4. Subjects the group to conditions of life that are intended to cause physical destruction of the group in whole or in part;
5. **Imposes measures intended to prevent births within the group;** Or
6. **Transfers by force children of the group to another group;** or attempts to do so shall be punished as provided in subsection (b).

Subsection (b) provides penalties of $1,000,000 fines and life imprisonment.

The recent practice of placing black infants with white families obviously comes under number 6 and is a phenomenon we should examine closely to ascertain whether we are doing more damage than good by virtue of this program. I am not suggesting this is so, but all too often when only a black child's welfare is involved the situation is not given enough thought or study. Now, consider line item number 5.

64

The U.S. District Court for the Eastern District of Missouri held (in February, 1994) that crack laws established by Congress which equate one gram of crack with 100 grams of powdered cocaine were inspired by "unconscious racism" and the judge refused to sentence the black youth.

Crack is bad. It has become the scourge of our nation's inner cities. But does that give Congress the right, via "unconscious racism," to commit "unconscious genocide?"

By enacting a law which they knew would impact almost exclusively on blacks (92 percent of prison inmates incarcerated for violating crack laws are black) they have removed a large percentage of young black men from society during their peak child-producing years. While it may be debatable if this was the direct intent of Congress, there can be no debating the fact that this is the result.

The system coerces middle-class blacks to go along with this mistreatment of young blacks by characterizing any opposition to the laws as being pro drugs or pro lawlessness; this, however, is just not the case. Blacks want to see drug use and its attendant violence brought under control as much as whites. But, by continuing to allow any members of our race to be imprisoned via the use of disparate laws which are unevenly enforced in favor of whites, we are giving our tactic approval to ill treatment. And if we allow our race to be ill-treated in one area it will continue to be ill-treated in others. Indeed, if the Department of Justice mistreats us, why should any other segment of American society do any differently?

Throughout our history in this country, we have been treated differently by the courts; we can't gain equality until we quit allowing ourselves to be treated as judicial punching bags.

Under Bill Clinton, nine of the ten men who have been sentenced to death under drug "kingpin" laws have been black. Only one white person was sentenced to death, although three-quarters of the drug kingpins convicted in federal courts are white.* It seems whites just can't commit a drug-related crime and be sentenced to death under federal laws.

A Justice Department spokesman stated to *USA Today* that Mary Lee Warren, the Deputy Assistant Attorney General, who reviews the death-penalty cases, "has no idea . . . what the race of the individuals is." If you buy that, I've got some prime swampland to sell you. *All* criminal

---

* See the article on this topic in *USA Today*, March 16, 1994.

documents indicate the criminal's race on them. Believe me, I've seen enough of them to know.*

But suppose we afford the Justice Department the benefit of the doubt. Say the race of the defendants is obliterated from the documents before they are sent to Washington for review. How then did nine out of ten turn out to be black? The answer the Justice Department spokesman would have you believe is that blacks are just more criminal in nature and therefore more deserving of the death penalty. But the real answer is quite obvious: with the exception of the odd white convict or two, only cases involving blacks are sent to Washington by the U.S. attorneys around the country for consideration. It's called selective prosecution. Whites' cases are mitigated down to the point where they are not subject to receiving Big Casino.

Two questions come to mind: One, what constitutes **SUBSTANTIAL** under the genocide laws? And two, who enforces the law when it is the government that is committing the crime?

How many young black men will be inequitably incarcerated before something is done about the crack laws? How many black kingpins will face the death penalty before the laws are applied equally across the board, irrespective of race?

Naturally no one in the Department of Justice is going to admit that what they are, and have been, doing to blacks in the name of the War on Drugs is "unconscious genocide," but then, neither did anyone in Hitler's government.

* On March 14, 1995 the Federal Government announced that it would execute its first prisoner, a white, in more than 30 years. The execution is scheduled for the end of March . . . and will probably be followed by the deaths of a number blacks at the hands of the Federal Government.

GUNS AND MADMEN

THE RECENT TRAGEDY on a Long Island-bound train again points up our desperate need for an effective means of controlling firearms. The Brady Bill, the largely symbolic first step Congress took in this direction, will do little to actually curb violence since so many guns are already in circulation. Someone bent on doing violence can readily purchase a weapon of devastation without going to a firearms dealer. Purchasing a gun in most American cities is about as hard as locating a neighborhood bar or liquor store. And no license or certification of sanity is required; all you need is the money.

The first reports on this incident stated that the perpetrator, a thirty-something-year-old black man, remained calm after his capture and showed no remorse for his heinous actions afterward. The initial reports didn't make mention of any history of mental illness, but such evidence would offer some small bit of solace to the grieving families and allay our fears for our own security a bit; after all, anything can be expected from a nut case.

Irrespective of whether or not the man has ever been hospitalized for mental problems, the enormity of his actions stands as mute testament to his obvious derangement. The increasing regularity of such incidents is, and well should be, cause for national alarm. Since it will be years before we realize any real benefit from newly enacted gun-control laws, it would serve us well to discern why more and more people are going around the final bend in their borderline lives.

The shooters in these incidents come in all colors, shapes, and sizes, so to categorize them is a bit more difficult, but not impossible. The one thing these walking time bombs have in common is great and deep-seated rage, caused by incidents real or imagined. We can do little to protect ourselves from those whose rage is imagined except provide hospitalization.

The others, who have never been diagnosed as dangerous, are the ones we have to concern ourselves with. While their acts never make sense to anyone but them, and under no circumstances can ever be justified, I can, however, understand how a person's mind can be so twisted by events that, in desperate revenge, one day they snap.

Thirty-two years ago, fresh out of high school, I went to work for a public-utility company whose work force had formerly been 99 percent white. After spending nearly ten years there and being given every reason to believe I too could realize the American Dream, I was told the time just wasn't right to promote any blacks beyond a certain point, no matter how qualified they might be. I know how ludicrous this now sounds but, in 1969, before civil-rights suits were used to address this type of racism, the general foreman thought nothing of telling me this in just those words. He also added he couldn't foresee a time when the climate would be conducive for such a move.

Needless to say, I was crushed. At age twenty-eight I was told I could go no higher, no matter how qualified or diligently I applied myself. My exemplary record left little doubt about my suitability for the job; even he admitted that much.

The rage which built up within me over the next six months frightened me. I would find myself daydreaming about positioning myself on the roof of the adjoining building and picking off the members of management who I felt had wronged me. Time caused this daydream to become more delicious as it passed.

Thank God I never acted on my daydream, and within the year I had quit the company, to protect my sanity, and maybe the lives of the other employees. In retrospect, I should have been able to cope with the situation better, but the point is, at the time the idea was very appealing to me. Luckily I was young enough to make a life for myself somewhere else, but if I had been fifteen or twenty years older I don't know how I would have felt. Placing individuals who feel life offers them limited options in a position where they become desperate is dangerous. Yet many supervisors at companies (the post office is a prime example) seem to take delight in tormenting those under them.

The shooter on the train was black; many others are white. But all of them carry around inside on a daily basis the rage many, many blacks have had to deal with for years. The amazing thing is more of them *don't* go off.

Unfairness in our society, typified by racial bias, is often to blame for pushing emotionally damaged people who are already on the edge, but would otherwise limp on through life, off the deep end into an act of madness. The callousness which racial prejudice breeds (although not limited to just race) causes us to treat each other abominably. Is it any wonder that some get mad as hell and decide they aren't going to take it anymore?

ALABAMA IS STILL ALABAMA

I'M DELIGHTED, thrilled, pleased as punch, gratified, and tickled pink (which, considering my melanotic hue, is pretty amazing) over the decision of a school board in a small Alabama town to reinstate a high school principal who had been suspended for espousing racist views and implementing bigoted policy.

The principal, whom the school superintendent had recommended to be fired, had threatened to cancel the senior prom if any interracial couples were planning to attend. When questioned about his edict by a senior female student, who has a black mother and a white father, as to what she should do, he sidestepped her question by stating "mistakes" like her was what his policy was designed to prevent in the future.

The reason I'm so elated over the school board's members' action is, by demonstrating in no uncertain terms racism is alive and well in Alabama, their insensitive vote should serve as a wakeup call to the black parents of the community. Maybe now they'll take a more active interest in the kinds of individuals who are teaching their children.

The high school in question has a student ratio of 63 percent black versus 37 percent white. That the school board had only one black member out of six indicates the black parents first should be angry with themselves. With the evidently high percentage of eligible black voters in town, it's obvious they just haven't been on their job. They have allowed a white minority to control the school system, and therefore the future of their children, out of tradition even though there had been previous accusations of racism concerning the principal. Even if things were going smoothly, they still should have taken more of an interest in the school careers of their children. Black parents everywhere have been deficient on this point for too long.

A few years ago a friend of mine got involved in her son's school program after he reported to her that he, as a senior at an all-black high school, was being given instruction in how to fill out a welfare application. Not a college application; not a job application—a welfare application. Evidently the white teacher who my friend eventually found had instituted the instruction felt the black students weren't going to have too much of a chance out there in the real world, or was simply projecting his own prejudices into the curriculum.

Recalling an incident from my own high-school days back in the Stone Age, a somewhat similar incident comes to mind. We had this ancient white chemistry teacher who constantly berated us about how dumb we were. And he felt he had plenty of proof, since not one of the thirty or so students had learned to balance a chemical equation after weeks of effort. One day the teacher, who was so old he had one foot in the grave and the other on a banana peel, was out sick and a little old lady (when you're sixteen everyone seems old) came in to substitute for him. When she asked what we were working on, we shamefully told her about the chemical equations none of us could balance. I had been somewhat suspicious all along about the method our teacher had been using for, while it was no surprise that I couldn't grasp the concept, I was amazed that Hilda and Harold, the class brainiacs, couldn't either.

The woman went to the blackboard and in fifteen minutes every student in the class was balancing equations like crazy! Obviously the old teacher, who I now realize was a racist (even if he didn't know it himself), had been making the work too difficult for us to comprehend so we would fit his preconceived concept of our intelligence level. A more charitable conclusion would be that he was simply a poor teacher, but in either case he shouldn't have been in the classroom. That he constantly called us dumb had hurt like hell, too.

We would like to believe anyone attracted to the high calling of teaching as a career is automatically above prejudice; sadly, such is just not the case. Some of them also fall victim to the "American Disease."

If the school board had fired the principal in Alabama, the whites in the community (who strongly supported him) would have been up in arms. However, only one white board member was willing to risk being called "nigger lover." If the vote had, by some miracle, gone against the principal I can readily imagine the whites breaking out their Confederate flags and holding parades down Main Street as they sang rousing choruses of "Dixie" in an attempt to intimidate the local blacks. I wonder how they would feel if they knew their favorite anthem was written by two black brothers, the Snowdens (sons of former slaves) because they missed the farm they'd been raised on in the South?

If American black parents don't organize, register, and vote in some board members who are more sensitive to their children's needs, they deserve whatever kind of racist they get saddled with.

BROWN V. BOARD OF EDUCATION

EVERYONE LOVES NATIONAL ANNIVERSARIES. We use these milestones to mark, measure, and celebrate many events in our history. In addition to providing us with a national sense of who we are, anniversary dates reassure us of the progress we've made as a nation since the original occurrence of the event. All except one.

1994 marks the fortieth anniversary of *Brown* v. *Board of Education.* This historic Supreme Court decision, which was supposed to strike down school segregation, marks the unofficial beginning of the modern Civil Rights movement as well.

This year virtually every national publication and many local publications (both black and white) have done retrospectives on this supposedly far-reaching decision. Of course television got into the act, trotting out much-worn footage of soldiers escorting black children through hostile white mobs to formerly all-white schools; governors blocking schoolhouse doors; and police dogs and water cannons being used against peaceful black protestors. Naturally the proud and determined black leaders of the era, from Thurgood Marshall to Rosa Parks to Martin Luther King Jr., were all profiled.

Certainly there has been progress. But when statistics prove that many school districts are more segregated now than they were in 1954, blacks realize how little of the progress has been real and lasting.

A few of the many articles I've read about the anniversary were written by blacks who trumpet how many black elected officials we now have, how many black quarterbacks, and how successful some blacks are doing at formerly all-white colleges, as if a gradual, incremental lifting of the jackboot of oppression off our necks, a partial granting of the rights we've been entitled to all along is sufficient to placate us and convince us to wait patiently for another forty years.

During the period that American blacks have won and lost gains, South Africa, which started from the point of official and avowed racism in the form of apartheid, has elected its first black president. Our Civil Rights movement still functions more on the level of style than substance, more rhetoric than real change, more show than actual progress. Forty years is an awfully long time to accomplish so damn little. The reason is simple. Blacks are given court decisions, civil-rights legislation, and presidential proclamations as if they actually mean something. Like the promises made to Native Americans more than a century ago via treaties which were promptly broken, the "landmark" promises to blacks implied in federal legislation and court decisions have proved to be a cruel hoax, an empty promise, and a dirty joke.

Not that the laws are unenforceable; they're merely unenforced. We always seem to win the court battles but lose the enforcement wars. And it has been thus ever since the Emancipation Proclamation.

At the end of the Civil War the North knew that southerners would resist any changes in the social order which would actually improve the lot of blacks. The Freedman's Bureau was put into place to insure these newly granted freedoms and rights were actually granted. The white officials of the Freedman's Bureau were first winked at and then outright ignored, similar to the rights of the newly enfranchised blacks, who often found themselves worse off than they were before they were freed. Not only didn't they get the promised forty acres, they didn't even get the mule! This set up a pattern which is still followed today.

The government makes new laws to insure fairness and racists promptly find a way to get around them. *While the government sits by and does absolutely nothing!* We've had adequate laws on the books to protect the rights of blacks and other minorities for years, but any fool knows an unenforced law is as bad, or worse, than no law at all.

Let anyone in any situation (excepting those where the rights of blacks are being violated) challenge the might of the federal government and see how far he gets. The power of the feds will rain down upon him until he is turned into dust if he doesn't submit to its authority. Look what happened to the Branch Davidians in Waco, Texas. Let any black step out of line and see what happens to him.

Schools, however, have been allowed to remain segregated, bankers are allowed to deny blacks loans for homes and other legitimate purposes, and employers have been allowed to discriminate on the basis of race and sex at will and with impunity, because they all know the laws against their illegal and immoral behavior aren't likely to be enforced in any manner. Racism exists in America because the federal government—which was responsible for it in the first place—does nothing meaningful about it.

If federal civil rights officials had a mind to, they could not only lead the horse of racism to the waters of fairness and equality, they could, with their awesome but unused power, also make it drink.

It's enough to make me very disenchanted with court victories like Brown *v.* Board of Education.

RADICAL EDUCATION REFORM

EVERYONE AGREES the largest cause of crime and violence is poverty. And the largest cause of poverty is a lack of adequate education which prepares youth to compete in a modern world.

Everyone agrees our education system is a shambles. Underfunded, overcrowded, and so violent many teachers should qualify for combat pay. However, anyone remotely familiar with our inner-city schools knows the majority of the disruption is instigated by a small minority of the students. Remove this small minority and the others will be better able to go with the business of education.

The basic trouble with our school systems is that they have failed to keep pace with changing society. What worked years ago won't work now. The only real changes have been in the erecting of metal detectors in even some elementary schools. This is now required because the age at which youngsters begin engaging in violent activities is falling lower and lower. At the rate we're going, we'll have to frisk kids going to preschool not too many years down the road.

The school officials can readily identify those students who are disruptive. The problem is, what to do about them? Someone is going to have to have the guts to say certain parents just aren't cutting it, in terms of providing their children with guidance, and move to create training schools, far removed from ghettos where these youngsters who are starting down the wrong road are sent.

At present we have juvenile facilities where wayward youth are sent that are little more than junior prisons. We have the bodies, and it is our fault if we don't educate their minds while we have them under our influence. The problem is these facilities were chartered as holding facilities first and foremost. Education has always been a low priority of the officials at these institutions. All that needs to change.

There is a simple way to do it. Education is compulsory until the age of sixteen in most states, but why only to sixteen, and why is only education compulsory? Why is completion of a certain course of study, which provides the youth with a marketable skill, not also mandatory? We *demand* that a child go to school to age sixteen. Why not *demand* that she obtain a skill which would provide her with employment before she is allowed to stop going? We are now in second and third generations of welfare children whose parents can't impart to them the value of education. Does that mean they need it less? They probably need it more. Society has a right to protect itself. By forcing youth, on pain of incarceration, to acquire a skill before they are let out into the world is a necessity today. Otherwise, as we already know, too many of them won't get one.

If they weren't going to wind up being wards of the state, via either prison or welfare, then society could let these youth do what they damn well please. Since society will eventually have to pick up the tab for these children's failure to obtain a decent education, then society has a right—nay, an obligation—to insure that everyone receives training so as not to become burdens on society.

Certainly this won't save all our youth; some will still fall through the cracks—but many more will, even if it's against their wills at first, be saved. The time will eventually come when graduating from high school or training school will be as accepted as the fact that a child has to stay in school to age sixteen. And if they know, early on, that their ticket out of school will have to be a completion certificate then they will apply themselves in a serious manner.

Speak to me not of civil liberties. What liberties do these children of the underclass have now? The liberty to drop out of school, deal drugs, shoot and kill each other, and then fill our prisons? No, it is up to us to require changes in the education system which reflect today's realities.

CULTURALLY RELEVANT PROGRAMS

THERE IS A crying need within the black race to develop new, culturally sensitive methods of dealing with the myriad racially based problems. Historically, what we have done to solve our problems was use models designed for, or at least by, whites. While these solutions may work very well for them, judging by the plight of one-third of the black race, they haven't worked too well for us.

The fact that we've used methods not designed for or considerate of our heritage is somewhat understandable. Since whites were, in the main, in control of these efforts, we went along with the methods they put forth, even though we often knew they would not, and could not, work. It is time we, and they, realize why these methods aren't working and attempt new and different ones. The past silence on the part of blacks was, and is, due to our gratitude that someone cared enough to attempt to solve the problems, no matter how ill-conceived the methods. We have been afraid of sounding like ingrates by protesting that the methods were doomed to failure.

Cultural differences, more than anything else, account for most of the failure of the programs. The route to success in America was, and is, thought to lie in being as much like whites as possible. Rather than take into account the differences between the races, attempts were made to make blacks as white as possible, hoping this would break down the barriers which have kept us out of the mainstream and relegated us to second-class citizenship.

The large pool of dissatisfied blacks in corporate America is mute testament to the failure of such thinking.

It is without malice, or with very little of it, that I state the time has come to admit blacks are never going to assimilate into the mainstream of white American life. While this statement may raise protests to the contrary, especially among those blacks from the last generation who still hold such hopes, let me be quick to add that this is not as bad as it once seemed. It is simply a reality which has to be dealt with forthrightly and honestly.

What this realization does is finally make blacks the architects of their own destiny. No longer should we wait, hat in hand, for America to decide how it wants to treat us. The thinking I advocate puts the majority of the responsibility for our advancement right where it belongs—on the shoulders of blacks.

White racism is, without a doubt, the cause of most of the conditions of the black underclass, but unfortunately whites who are unwilling to admit the extent of racism in this country, or the effects it has upon the black race, aren't going to solve the problems they have created. We can spin our wheels forever demanding that white America admit its guilt and debt to the black race. Enough of them have already done so without any net effect on institutionalized racism. This exercise in futility does little to solve our present-day problems. No, the only thing for us to do is to write off the sweat equity we've invested for the last 300 years into the building of this nation as an uncollectible bad debt.

There are some self-help measures we can make as a race which probably would receive some assistance (other than just welfare payments) from the federal government. However, these programs would have to be initiated by blacks *for* blacks. There now exist enough black social scientists to address the problems of the race. Granted, many of them are so far removed from those problems (and the people who have them) as to be rendered almost ineffective. But there still are others who, having maintained closer ties to their roots, realize any programs which ultimately prove successful will have to take into account cultural differences and the need for those differences to be addressed.

During the sixties, white youth experimented in communal living. While some of the attempts were successful for a sustained period, most were not. This is a way of life blacks have been successful at for centuries and which could offer some solutions to today's problems of the underclass. The thing is, the government just isn't designed to foster these types of living and working arrangements. The traditional nuclear family of a mother, father, and any number of children is more than an established fact; it is the only accepted American lifestyle.

When blacks and others do make attempts at alternative lifestyles it is usually under the aegis of a religious nut and eventually turns into a cult. This doesn't have to happen. Lifestyles which are more compatible with the temperaments of blacks should be explored as a means of addressing the pressing problems of the underclass.

FEWER BLACKS IN COMMERCIALS

ONE VERY UNSCIENTIFIC MEASURE of how well blacks are faring in America is by noting how visible minorities are in television commercials. For years blacks were virtually ignored by sponsors who evidently took for granted that minorities would buy their products . . . even if they weren't represented in ads.

During the eighties this attitude changed as national and international purveyors of fast food, soft drinks, and other highly competitive products realized a new generation of blacks wouldn't continue to patronize their goods and services while remaining underrepresented in their commercials. The sponsors didn't come to this conclusion on their own but had to be coerced by black civic and economic organizations into making their ads more reflective of the diversity which is America.

Not all of the advertisers, however, got the message for it is still fairly common to see smaller or regional advertisers air commercials which still feature whites only. And some of the larger advertisers, once they felt the "heat" was off during the latter years of the Reagan-Bush era, tended to revert to their racist ads. We have to remain vigilant since we know how strongly the images projected on the television screen can impact on our youth.

One direct-marketing company based in Atlanta, for example, evidently feels blacks and other minorities don't use telephones since their ad for a telephone headset (which frees up the hands for other tasks) features at least a half dozen different people in various situations using the product—all of them white.

A more serious measure of how the depth of racism in America is reflected on the small screen can be seen in the advertising done by a number of social organizations concerned with funding for such issues as public education and health. These ads are produced by groups which have historically been considered very liberal in terms of race relations, and are designed to convince the average American viewer to become more supportive of the programs which these groups endorse: the need for more of our resources to be directed into the areas of public education and universal health care.

When I first noticed the dearth of people of color (the few minorities who are featured are so fair-complected and are seen so briefly one is left to wonder if they are seen at all) in their advertising I became alarmed. If blacks can't get fair treatment from these liberal organizations where can they receive it? Then it hit me. These groups weren't being biased, but quite the opposite. The creators of the ads realize America is so racist they feel their chances of getting the response and support they're seeking from predominantly white America will be enhanced if no, or few, black faces are seen in the ads. They fear white backlash. They assume that whites won't be inclined to support causes which will benefit blacks. Therefore, their thinking goes, include as few blacks as they can get away with in the commercials.

Since I'm not privy to the decision-making process of these advertisers, I'm only surmising this scenario. Surely some folks will say I'm merely paranoid and ascribing deeper, sinister motives to innocuous situations or oversights. I sincerely hope those who might hold this view are correct. But, like the Rodney King incident, where blacks were told they weren't actually seeing what they thought they were seeing, I know what I see.

Ah, the quandaries one encounters being black in America at the close of the twentieth century! How am I to react if my perception of the situation is accurate? Do I protest for more blacks to be included in the commercials, knowing in my heart the creators of the virtually all-white ads are right in their assessment of the possibility of white backlash? Or do I take the more pragmatic position of "it's better if we're not seen if this will increase the funding for programs which will aid blacks"? What, gentle reader, would you do?

Since my momma didn't raise no fools, I'll have to remain silent on this issue and just accept the nearly all-white ads.

WHAT'S UP WITH THE COVERAGE?

I THOUGHT CRIME WAS A HOT ISSUE. According to the many stories in both print and electronic media it is the number-one issue on the minds of most Americans. Yet, when a group of high-profile black leaders met in Washington in early January, 1994 under the aegis of Jesse Jackson's Rainbow Coalition to address the issue media coverage was scant indeed.

Only *USA Today* did a feature on the beginning of the conference, and then it relegated the conclusions reached by the conferees (some of which were very important to solving the problem of crime) to page eight, four days later. It seems as though the fact of crime is much more important to the media than viable solutions which blacks can offer.

It is well understood that the rise in concern over crime is largely media-generated and reflects Americans' concern with rising unemployment. The worse off the average citizen is, the more inclined he is to focus on crime. The public is always looking for a whipping boy to take its frustrations out on, and, as usual, issues which impact on blacks are the most likely targets.

This is not to say there isn't a very serious problem with crime which has to be dealt with in the black community; there certainly is. Why then wasn't the crime conference given more coverage? Many blacks have long felt the problems of the underclass are only of concern to whites when the violence moves out of the black neighborhoods and affects them in some way. Black-on-black crime has never particularly disturbed whites, this reasoning goes. And this logic, in the face of the media's recent refusal to cover a conference by concerned blacks, makes this thinking even harder to refute. It seems America doesn't care to hear about what it did to create the problem (and what it should do to really solve it), only how many people are going to be locked up in *hopes* of solving it.

The recent round of tougher laws, which culminated in new criminal sanctions being enacted in California on March 7, 1994, was largely inspired by the media attention to a heinous kidnapping/murder of a young girl in the northern part of the state. Any senseless loss of a young life is tragic and every heart goes out to the parents of the child. However, enacting a law which can land someone in prison for twenty-five years for something as relatively innocuous as being convicted three times of writing bad checks will do little to prevent this sort of crime. Also, the fact that black youths have, for years, been dying every day by the score without any similar outrage from authorities is further proof of the lack of value placed on black lives by society.

Many incarcerated blacks shake their heads in amazement and disgust as they watch whites convicted of rapes and murders treated relatively lightly by prison authorities and the parole system simply because they are white, while they, because they are black, languish in prison convicted of far less serious crimes. Statistics reveal blacks serve 50 percent longer sentences for the same crime than whites. If America is really concerned about the release of dangerous convicts, then it should address the racism which is so prevalent within the prison parole systems. The tougher the laws become, the more the whites in charge of the system feel no white person should be subjected to the full brunt of them and invent unique methods to assure they are not. Racism doesn't stop at the prison gate.

Our citizenry is constantly and shamelessly manipulated by the media. Trumpeting crime sells better than spotlighting solutions. The failure of the media to cover the crime conference is due in part to the fact that whites don't want to hear how the racist system they maintain is largely responsible for the high crime rate. Rather than confront their racism and attempt to come to terms with it they would rather stay in denial and spend untold billions of dollars attempting to disprove the fact that crime is, more than anything else, a function of the conditions they have created in the underclass. And the media willingly goes along with this sham.

FIRED BY THE FEDS

AN ARTICLE by Stephen Barr in the *Washington Post*'s weekly national edition (February 21 to 27, 1994) details how blacks working for the federal government are fired at a rate three times that of their white coworkers. In the fiscal year of 1992, 12,000 federal employees were fired, of which 52 percent were black, although blacks comprise only 28 percent of the federal workforce.

The article goes on to state a number of studies of the phenomenon are underway. The feds, evidently, will leave no stone unturned to discover what blacks already know: racism is alive and flourishing in every segment of American life. The federal government will spend untold millions of dollars to eventually come up with a report the size of the Manhattan phone book which will attempt to couch the "newly discovered" racism in more acceptable language.

Since the article further states most of the firings occur at the lower employment levels among newer employees (many of whom are still on first-year probation) the report will probably state in fedspeak, "entry-level federal employees of the minority persuasion are encountering an enhanced level of difficulty adjusting to, and successfully interacting with, the existent hierarchy in their new workplace situations than their white counterparts." Translation: they can't deal with a racist boss.

The fact that most of the problems occur at the point where entry-level workers come face-to-face with their immediate supervisors is not surprising. This is the level where cultures usually clash. A small-minded, white, frontline supervisor, who has worked his way one step up the ladder often will attempt to throw his weight around with the new employees in general and with minority employees in particular. The new minority employee, who may be from the ghetto where putting up with racist white folks isn't a way of life, isn't about to take any Klan-type crap. Any black who has worked in an entry-level job knows the drill.

The Equal Employment Opportunity Commission may be able to force the government and others to hire blacks and other minorities, but it has been reluctant, especially since the Reagan-Bush era, to enforce rules of fair treatment on the job.

Once, many years ago, I ran a "pre-employment" training class at the virtually all-white public-utility company I worked at in Cleveland, Ohio. The government had told the company to integrate its workforce or suffer the consequences. The senior managers of the company were becoming increasingly disturbed by the fact that they were putting twenty young blacks into fully paid "pre-employment" training programs and winding up with only two or three of the blacks left at the end of the six-week period. My supervisor asked me to assist in the program, hoping my presence would up their retention percentage. I declined three or four times over a six-month period until they finally met my terms and allowed me to run the entire program without any assistance or interference.

On the first day I simply told the twenty assembled young black men that while the higher-ups in the company really didn't mind them being there, the frontline supervisors, whom they would come into contact with, took an entirely different point of view. They viewed it as their sworn duty to make it as tough as possible for blacks to keep their jobs. They would allow them to be late without excuse or reason and not show up at all until they had accumulated a poor record that would justify firing them. They had to do two things if they wanted the job: be there, and be there on time.

While I was supposed to be teaching them rudimentary math, I was also teaching them how to "play past" the racial slurs they would encounter, at least until they were past their probationary period. After they saw how I would ridicule any white coworker unmercifully if they dared make a racial slur in my presence, they caught on to the game. They knew they too would, after six months, be able to defend themselves the same way.

At the end of the six-week period, I had nineteen of the twenty still on the job. During the next couple of years, I ran hundreds of new employees through the program successfully, and in the process dispelled the notion that blacks were unqualified or incapable of performing the duties of the entry-level jobs. Contrary to the illusion whites have created for years, most entry-level positions can be handled by virtually anyone who is afforded the training and is willing to work.

I taught them how to ignore the racists until they had enough seniority on the job to be able to give them a good cussing out without getting fired. Maybe someone should teach newly hired federal employees the same thing.

PAY NOW OR PAY LATER

REPARATION FOR THE WORK performed by blacks during slavery, while on its face is a legitimate concept, has never seriously, for a couple of reasons, captured the public's imagination. Chief among them is the fact that few blacks ever gave these payments (which were paid to Americans of Japanese descent unjustly interred during World War II) a ghost of a chance of being made.

The logical reasoning put forth by Japanese-Americans was, "why were second- and third-generation American-born Japanese locked up while German immigrants, who had arrived in this country immediately prior to the outbreak of the war (and were far more likely to be spies), allowed to remain free?" But Uncle Sam, when it comes to how blacks are treated in this country, is like a deadbeat relative—he may know he owes you, but he's just not going to pay. Second is the matter of how much to whom. There were some free blacks during slavery (not many, but some) whose descendants would not qualify for payment. Any black Americans who pressed the government for such payments would probably be told *their* ancestors (surprise, surprise) actually were among the few free blacks. The government would no doubt come up with the documentation to prove it. Also, their reasoning would be any payments which amounted to anything more than tokenism would be cost-prohibitive. However, the lack of ways and means to implement such a program doesn't negate the fact that blacks are owed a debt for past services rendered.

The magnitude of the problems many, especially young, blacks face at present, in terms of crime, violence, and poverty, will require a huge infusion of cash and commitment. It may be appropriate for blacks to attempt to convince the government to look at these expenses in terms of a form of reparation. If the problems of the underclass are to be adequately addressed, that is, if the real root causes of poverty and crime are going to be attacked, then a number of programs will have to be developed.

And blacks are going to have to take an active role in the solving of these problems. We are going to have to volunteer our time to assist in managing the programs. If the staffing of these programs is left solely to government bureaucrats then the results will probably be disastrous. While the government should assist in the costs of running the programs, it should be up to blacks to provide the people who will be needed to shepherd the youth of our race to a better tomorrow.

The Job Corp is a program which has attempted to rescue many inner-city youths from desolate futures. Imagine how much more successful it could be if more members of the community at large are involved? The problem with programs which are run entirely by bureaucrats is they lack heart and soul. Even the most dedicated staffers eventually come to see their mission as just another job rather than the rescuing of members of the underclass. It takes ordinary, everyday citizens, imbued with missionary zeal, to inculcate the values we wish to instill in our youth. Blacks will have to lend a hand or be satisfied with the job the government does, or doesn't, do.

Some of the at-risk youth will be able to be assisted by outreach programs run by local churches, but for others the neighborhoods they live in are so bad, no amount of intervention will suffice to overcome the negative influences. For these youths, the only solution is to move them to other environments as it's seemingly impossible to rid ourselves of ghettos. For those not raised in a ghetto it is too easy to say the conditions can be overcome with proper intervention; this just isn't always so. When these children are having to duck bullets going to and from school, and wonder if a slug will tear through their bedroom walls at night, no amount of local programs can help. Two or three hours a day spent in a safe situation doesn't cancel out the other nervous hours spent in the ghetto.

The only realistic solution is to remove these children, starting with pregnant teenage mothers and then moving up the age brackets, to safe Children's Camps located perhaps on recently closed military bases. There, in a safe environment free from drugs and violence, the children can be molded into responsible citizens. The underclass could be wiped out in a generation if we take the initiative and make a program like this a reality. This solution certainly isn't ideal, but, compared to the options we're faced with, it may be the only one available. Anything less is addressing the problem piecemeal. Since society already pays all of the costs of feeding and housing many of the at-risk youth through welfare payments and other social programs, it is simply a matter of paying for this care in another, safer environment. We're going to have to pay one way or the other, either through solving the problems of how these youths are raised, or the cost of incarcerating them for a good portion of their lives as adults. The choice is ours: pay now or pay later.

HUMAN RIGHTS

IT WILL NO DOUBT TAKE a complete reordering of America's priorities for blacks to achieve full equality in "The Land of the Free and the Home of the Brave."

The exceedingly accurate title of Lani Guinier's book *The Tyranny of the Majority* eloquently describes blacks' condition in America. It is a tyranny which doesn't seem to disturb our government nearly as much when it occurs to citizens here as when it occurs to citizens of other countries.

Currently our government is debating whether to apply a financial hammerlock on mainland China to force the repressive government there to improve its record on human-rights abuses. We're using the carrot and stick of "most favored nations trading status" to coerce the authoritarian government there to release certain political prisoners and to improve the lot of those remaining incarcerated.

Amnesty International has documented the less-than-adequate conditions which exist in China for dissidents but can't make the same unbiased assessment of conditions in America's prisons, since ours is the only government of the so-called "free" world which doesn't allow this well-respected organization inspection rights within its borders.

Card sharks, charlatans, and mountebanks the world over know the trick of the red card. In a game called Three Card Monte, the object is to keep the sucker watching the red card as he is being fleeced. U.S. foreign policy works in much the same way. We run all over the world criticizing other nations for how they treat their citizens while continuing to commit human-rights violations on a large percentage of blacks and other minority Americans both in and out of prison. Our red card of concern is only a mask to keep others from making the same charges against our government that we are so quick to make against them.

Another playing-card metaphor also comes to mind to describe America's supposed concern for human rights: one-eyed jacks. Of the four jacks in a deck of cards, two are facing front so both eyes can be seen, while the other two are facing so that only one eye is exposed, as if there were something to hide. And with American foreign policy, there certainly is.

We hide the fact, or at least attempt to hide it, that our foreign policy is based on nothing more than complete self-interest. Which is a perfectly legitimate basis for us to conduct affairs with other nations of the world, if we didn't constantly pretend to higher altruistic motives.

If Bosnia were filled with oil instead of strategically unimportant mountain ranges, we would have been in there brokering a solution or kicking a little butt. But Bosnia had nothing to offer which would add to our national wealth so we sat passively by and allowed the killing to continue unchecked.

Red China is potentially the largest untapped consumer market left in the world. 1.2 billion people with few televisions, autos, washing machines, refrigerators, or other capitalist creature comforts is enough to make American businessmen salivate; and they have been.

Our corporate types are planning to raid the joint. They have been chomping at the bit to get in on the ground floor before Japan, Germany, and South Korea—none of which has a need to attempt to rehabilitate China up to their standards before doing business—gobble up all of the lucrative markets. They're afraid that by the time we quit playing this fraudulent holier-than-thou game the country will have already been plucked as clean as a Peking duck.

The heads of American companies already doing some business in China have been attempting to convince the state department that the best way to insure the human rights of the dissidents is to let free enterprise take its course. Their logical conclusion is, once the have-nots, whom the dissidents represent, have something, there will no longer be a need for dissent. They will all be co-opted by the new prosperity. And the businessmen are dead right.

The same situation exists in this country. Blacks can be co-opted out of the behavior which brings them into conflict with the authorities simply by allowing them to participate fully in the economic bounty of America.

America should stop the hypocritical rhetoric and practice at home what it preaches to every other country of the world. Respect for human rights begins at home. The most frightening aspect of the situation in this country is that America has become inured to the suffering of its black citizens; it no longer considers what it is doing to us as violations of world standards of decency.

NIPPING HATE IN THE BUD

A CHILLING STORY about violence was aired on *60 Minutes* on June 5, 1994. A number of white high school and college-age youths—composed of both males and females—had banded together in their suburban Los Angeles community to form a neo-Nazi skinhead group.

The few leaders of the now-defunct group who were willing to be interviewed on camera stated that they had become weary of being targeted for intimidation by black and Latino gangs in their multiracial neighborhood. They told stories of being taunted by racial slurs in high school, such as being called "white bread" and "cracker." While this must have been unpleasant for them, it doesn't excuse what they planned in retaliation.

Not content just to form a self-protection group, the youths, numbering about twenty, soon began taking aggressive action against their perceived tormentors. They randomly selected lone blacks or Latinos and subjected them to a little roughing up. Soon, feeling empowered by mob psychology and poisoned by hate literature they had somehow gotten their hands on, they moved on to bigger, more audacious crimes. They learned to make pipe bombs which they tossed at a few select targets and desecrated a synagogue or two; standard fare for groups of this ilk. They began plotting a strategy to bring about a race war. They selected as their target the prominent minister of a large black Los Angeles congregation and concocted plans to kill him as he preached one Sunday morning. Their diabolical scheme called for them also to throw pipe bombs into the congregation and spray it with automatic weapon fire—for good measure, I guess.

However, the group had been infiltrated by the FBI. Two agents, posing as members of an established white hate group, won their confidence and convinced them to hold their meetings in a large storage room used to store Nazi paraphernalia. Naturally, the room was equipped with a couple of cameras to gather evidence of the group's activities.

The FBI warned the minister of the plot and he grudgingly took additional security precautions for the sake of his congregation. He refused, however, to turn his church into an armed camp.

Once the federal prosecutor handling the case felt he had enough evidence on the group to gain convictions, the three leaders were arrested by the FBI. One leader was convicted of bombing and sentenced to eight years in federal prison. The legal fate of the other two wasn't discussed on the program.

The prosecutor, supposedly sickened by the hateful rhetoric captured by the hidden cameras, set up a program to counsel the other youths. Since they called themselves skinheads he named the program "Grow Hair." He enlisted the black minister who was scheduled to be the target of their hateful violence to engage in a dialogue with the youths. The *60 Minutes* camera captured part of one of the sessions for its audience.

A group of ministers told the youths—among other things—that while they had the right to hate the ministers, they had no right to do violence to them. The session ended mawkishly with hugs all around, à la Oprah, Phil, Sally Jessy, et al.

The now-imprisoned former leader of the group was interviewed and offered his well-timed tears; indeed, he is a changed person after ten months of incarceration. He of course now sees the errors of his ways, and can't wait to get back out into society so he can show the world how much he has changed. Evidently no one has yet informed him that his sentence is nonparolable.

The prosecutor who set up the program was interviewed last. He was asked by Jane Pauley if he thought the program did any good. The man hemmed and hawed, but wouldn't say flat out if he had been successful or not. Who can tell in a situation like this? I, though, was waiting for a question from Jane Pauley which I knew wouldn't be forthcoming: what if these youths had been black or Latino? Would a program have been set up to show them the errors of their ways, or would they all have been convicted of conspiracy (of which the prosecutor had ample evidence) and all given long, long, prison sentences? In fact, was the program conceived of by the prosecutor just so he could avoid prosecuting these white youths and ruining their lives?

Come on, you know the answer to at least the first part. The leader (who would have been branded the most dangerous terrorist since Attila the Hun) would have received life without parole. After all, they didn't just *talk* about throwing bombs; they actually *threw* them. I don't know of a bomber in a federal prison who didn't receive a minimum of forty years. Those adjudged least culpable would have received ten years each, minimum.

Is this what I think these white youths should have received? No, of course not. While their actions were more than a mere childhood prank, the compassion shown by the prosecutor in an attempt to save some youngsters from a life of crime and hate was appropriate. My point is, black or Latino youths would not have received the same humane and life-saving treatment at the hands of a federal prosecutor. They would have been viewed only as twenty additional notches on his conviction belt—nothing more.

PART

III

DOWN BY LAW

THE COST OF BRUTALITY

POLICE BRUTALITY IS the idiot stepchild of the criminal-justice system. While it is normally kept well hidden from view, it occasionally is exposed to the light of day by such incidents as the Rodney King affair. Whenever these dark deeds reach the headlines, the police practitioners hunker down, circle the wagons, and wait for the publicity to blow over. They know the matter will soon fade from the public consciousness and it will once again be business as usual.

Unfortunately, one or two incidents a year (or 100 or 200) are not enough to stir those in authority to make any meaningful changes to the manner in which some law-enforcement officers relate to minorities. Brutality under color of authority has, for years, been an accepted method of relating to blacks, and senior officers, although they are quick to state the incidents are an aberration, are not willing to rock the boat by doing anything to prevent the violence. If they do, as they say, make changes the results are not yet evident to blacks. Blacks from every social class and walk of life know these self-serving statements are falsehoods of the most patent variety, but we seem to be at a loss to do anything about these incidents but complain.

Even though the number of officers who actually engage in this type of behavior is small, and it is as sickening to a majority of police officers as it is to the general public, the number of officers who, by their silence, condone this type of activity is not. The right-thinking officers are too quick to take refuge behind the "wall of blue" which requires—nay, demands—their silence. Preventing blacks from receiving a beating just isn't worth risking their careers, or even the enmity of their coworkers.

And though most of the guilty officers feel they can do their misdeeds and successfully hide behind their badges to escape punishment, and they all too often do, that doesn't mean there isn't a price to be paid. Their mistreatment of young blacks goes a long way towards creating the anger which these youths take out on their white victims when committing crimes. Their feelings often are, "We may not be able to get you, but we're going to take it out on *some* white person!" And sadly, all too often they do, with a vengeance.

Officers who brutalize citizens speciously tell themselves they are teaching a black youth a lesson by pummeling him; they actually think this will make him less inclined to commit a crime. But what it actually does it make him *more* prone to violent crime.

The problem of course is: who polices the police? In Jamaica many years ago, they had a problem with snakes so they imported the mongoose to contain it, which they did. Now they have a problem with the mongoose. If America was truly concerned with reducing the level of violence, we would conduct sting operations to deter police from brutalizing black citizens. Black agents from the FBI would be used as decoys in cities which have a known reputation for police brutality. Once this fact of life became known to police officers they would quickly modify their behavior.

However, since I seriously doubt any such effort is soon forthcoming, the duty to protect blacks from police brutality falls to our national civil-rights organizations. OPERATION COP WATCH should be instituted in major cities which have experienced this problem. Blacks armed with cameras should patrol the streets of their neighborhoods (accompanied by a lawyer or law student) and make a film of police and their methods. Where the problem is particularly bad, young blacks could be used as decoys to see how the police treat them in various situations.

The object of these groups wouldn't be to catch police while they are doing wrong, but to prevent them from doing wrong, because someone may be watching. However, as simple and potentially effective as this idea seems, I seriously doubt if civil-rights organizations will implement it since they historically react rather than act. This, I'm afraid, is a bit too radical for their passive blood, but that fact doesn't mean it isn't viable and necessary.

If violence in our country is to be reduced, it will have to be reduced on all sides. The howl set up by police from coast to coast would be deafening, but it would give blacks some sense of protection and the feeling someone is taking seriously their right to not suffer brutality.

Selective Enforcement

AMERICA'S CONUNDRUM concerning crime continues unabated. A White House aide, quoted in *Newsweek* (November 6, 1993), stated, "We don't know what causes crime. We have very little idea how to deter it." At least the aide was being candid. Part of the solution to the problem lies in others being equally honest.

In writing an essay about crime, I have to remain mindful of attempting to maintain my credibility, especially when I tackle an aspect of the root causes of crime no one wants to hear about. My aim is to approach the subject in as balanced a manner as possible, lest my position be dismissed as sour grapes or bitter carping. I would ask the reader to accept as fact my strong desire to help in reducing crime, and while they may not wish to hear some of the things I have to say, my not saying them won't make them any less true. With that caveat in place, I'll now attempt to shed some much-needed light onto one of the dark corners of crime.

In the eighties, Al Pacino starred in a film entitled *And Justice for All*. He portrayed an attorney fed up with the callous unfairness of the criminal-justice system. Although the film was darkly humorous, it was also deadly accurate. The whole system is riddled with inequities. Attempting to arrest crime with a faulty and badly flawed criminal-justice system is akin to attempting to build a house with a broken hammer and saw, or play music on a busted instrument; it simply can't be done.

I realize any enterprise as large as our combined state and federal justice systems is going to have some blemishes; that can't be helped. No system is perfect. But when the system is so flawed that its shortcomings actually perpetuate the problem it is supposed to deter, it's time to reexamine it. However, since the problems are so rooted and long-standing, I seriously wonder if anything can be done about them. The fact that the flaws inhibit the reduction of crime forces me to speak out nonetheless.

99

Let's start at the beginning with selective enforcement. As onerous as the subject is, and as much as the general public would like to believe it doesn't happen, unfortunately, it does. And it increases crime. *USA Today* (July 23, 1993) headlined a story which stated blacks were six times as likely to go to jail for the same behavior as whites, in relation to drug usage and sales. In one community, they were forty-six times as likely to go to jail as whites. Another story (out of Los Angeles) tells how a criminal defense attorney tracked the cases of 100 small-time drug dealers, 90 of whom were black, the other 10 white. The county prosecutor found a flaw in all of the ten whites' cases which caused him to dismiss them. All ninety of the blacks were prosecuted. I could relate stories from my own experiences (most blacks can) which bear these two examples out.

Selective enforcement increases crime in two ways. One, it allows some criminals to return to the streets to commit more crimes, now more secure in the knowledge they won't suffer any penalties; and, two, it creates a deeper lack of respect for the law among those who witness this favoritism. For some strange reason the police and court officials who practice this form of blatant racism, even though they oftentimes are very open about it, seem to think no one is taking notice of it, but blacks are.

This openness is indicative of two more things, the first being the practice is so widespread it is deemed by those in charge as acceptable; and, secondly, they know no one will listen to the complaints of the criminals who witness this anyway. And if anyone does complain he is dismissed as just looking for some reason to exculpate his own guilt. The truth is, the practice has been going on so long many young blacks are not outwardly upset by its use. They simply accept it as part of how things are. But on a deeper level, incidents such as these are what hardens young men into disrespectful felons.

GETTING GUNS
OFF THE STREETS

ALTHOUGH THE BRADY BILL is a step in the right direction, even its most ardent supporters realize it's largely a symbolic step at best. It, and other measures being taken by local communities around the country, will over time dry up the supply of firearms on the street, but that will be a long, slow process and does little to solve the immediate problem.

Occasionally over the years, and again during Christmas of 1993 in New York and Atlanta, weapons buy-back programs were launched. Considering the shortness of the duration of the programs, they have to be considered successes. While many of the people who turned in weapons for cash weren't themselves criminals, the fact remains there are now fewer guns on the street and in homes where burglars can steal them. Police know many, if not most, of the weapons used by youthful offenders in violent crimes are stolen. Maybe the burglar doesn't use the weapon but it is bought and sold, bought and sold, until it finds its way into the hands of someone who will use it.

In view of the success of the two programs, it would seem the authorities would be eager to expand them into standing offers by every police department in the country, or the Alcohol, Tobacco, and Firearms division of the U.S. Justice Department, with no questions asked. In addition the programs could be augmented in a manner which would get still more guns off the street. The authorities should issue an active bounty on guns. Let it be known that people can make themselves some money by buying guns, say at 100 dollars each, and selling them to the police for 200. The police may just be surprised at how many guns would soon turn up. There are some residents of the nation's ghettos who have an uncanny ability to come up with anything on which a dollar can be turned. They should be utilized in our efforts to get guns off the street.

In New York during the seventies, the police had a squad of officers whose sole purpose was to get guns off the street. They rode around town and stopped cars they thought they might find guns in. These basically illegal searches raised few cries from the citizenry or civil liberties groups because of the manner in which they were carried out. The officers stuck to their purpose: they didn't ask to see driver's licenses or registrations; they didn't ask harassing and illegal questions about where the drivers were coming from or going; if they spotted a bag of weed in the car during the search, they ignored it; and if they found a gun, they simply took it. In short, they wanted guns off the streets and nothing else. If no gun was found they thanked the occupants for their cooperation and allowed them to journey on unmolested. What raises a howl today (and it should) is the fact that police use the cover and excuse of searching for weapons to stop people and treat them like runaway slaves.

The need to stop and search for guns, even though the random stops are probably illegal, is a necessary evil. In the face of the mounting death toll from firearms, as long as the stops don't turn into a method for the police to beef up their arrest quotas, we should support them. But when officers proceed on constitutionally shaky grounds, and then abuse their authority by flagrantly suspending rights, this diminishes citizens' willingness to cooperate. And eventually civil liberties groups will get involved, fearful of how far the police will overstep their bounds.

This "us against them" mentality which is so prevalent in our nation's police departments probably hinders a bounty-for-guns program, since it doesn't conform to their notions of how guns should be taken off the streets—by kicking both butts and doors. They too often prefer to use their methods, regardless of how ineffective they are, simply for the excitement provided. Having people walk in with guns is too easy.

While many may take exception to the last two statements, I would venture to guess they would be hard pressed to come up with a good reason to not implement the program. When one considers how much havoc can be wrought on society by just one gun, 200 dollars a piece certainly isn't too high a price to pay.

THE NEED FOR CURFEWS

CURFEWS FOR MINORS can be an effective means of reducing violence if they are wisely and properly used. However, that is a big "if." Certainly young people who are accustomed to roaming around the streets at will at all hours of the night will rebel at being forced to stay indoors, unless they have a valid reason to be out. But, in spite of their likely protests, society has a right and duty to protect itself and youngsters who are at home at night can't commit crimes.

To further insure the success of curfews, parents should be held punitively accountable for the whereabouts of their minor offspring during curfew hours. Unless someone other than the juvenile is held responsible, the only result will be overworked police officers who will soon abandon their efforts—if not in policy, certainly in fact. Some young people will continue to break the curfew and gladly suffer whatever consequences are in store for them. However, if parents are subject to fines for their children's behavior the cry of "I just can't do anything with this child" will be heard far less.

Back to the "if." Unfortunately, all too often, police tend to use strengthened legal tactics, such as curfews, as a means of coming down indiscriminately on the citizens of the ghettos. They perceive the adoption of stiffer measures as also giving them license to use draconian—and sometimes Nazi-like—methods. In the long run, enforcing necessary laws in an unnecessary manner always proves to be counterproductive, if for no other reason than tensions are increased in the neighborhood.

Civil libertarians are ever mindful of police using whatever reasons they can conjure up to employ extralegal procedures under the guise of "combating crime." Often the American Civil Liberties Union and other champions of the Constitution object to curfews and other martial-law types of measures in a knee-jerk manner, but one which is based, to some degree, on past experiences. They fear that if these measures aren't challenged, others of an even harsher type will soon follow.

The public is going to have to accept as fact that there are some young police officers who could more aptly be called "peace-breakers" than "peace-keepers." They view their nightly tour of duty in black ghettos more as safaris, a chance to "hunt" black youth. They crave excitement and seek out opportunities—in many cases creating confrontational situations—to bust some heads. This attitude is not consistent with "peace-keeping."

It may be that different criteria for measuring the success of police need to be developed. Instead of how many arrests are made, maybe they should be judged by how peaceful their patrol area remains. As long as police promotions are based on the number of dangerous encounters an officer successfully handles, the officers will tend to attempt to create vehicles for climbing up the ranks. This is not to suggest that police should coddle criminals; just quit treating all blacks as if they were lawbreakers. Officers certainly have a right and duty to go home safely to their families at the end of their shifts. And they also have the right to use whatever force is necessary to do so. But whitewashing every violent police/citizen confrontation just won't wash any longer. The plain fact is, not every white officer is racially sensitive enough to patrol black areas. Many of them are still bringing built-in prejudices to work with them. Those who can't be re-trained have no business in the black community.

Curfews, which would make black neighborhoods safer, should be given serious consideration. The mostly white, concerned members of civil liberties organizations go home to safe neighborhoods at the end of the day; blacks deserve to be able to do the same. If it takes measures which make these well-meaning defenders of the Constitution uncomfortable to achieve this in black neighborhoods, so be it. As the situation now stands, the only rights many young blacks now possess is the right to die young.

What is needed is a method of insuring that the police don't take a necessary technique which could reduce crime in the ghetto and use it for other, more sinister ends. Blacks shouldn't be denied safe neighborhoods because of fear of police adopting more oppressive measures. Maybe the civil liberties organizations should concentrate more of their efforts on helping blacks assure police aren't brutalizing minorities rather than suggest black youth be allowed to continue to run amok in our neighborhoods for the sake of the Constitution.

CASES OF CORRUPTION?

THE RECENT ARREST of a number of top black police officials in Washington, D.C., is not surprising. The FBI targets many high-ranking black officials, elected, appointed, and those who have come up through civil service, for prosecution. The FBI assumes black officials are more prone to accept bribes and engage in other criminal activity, and they like easy targets. In private, FBI officials derisively state that black officials are morally inferior to their white counterparts, are all dope fiends, and therefore are rightly targeted for extra investigation attention. These officials gloss over the misdeeds of white officials until they have no other choice but to investigate, and often then the results are a whitewash.

The fact that most blacks, elected or not, feel the system is stacked against them (a provable fact) is accountable for any difference in the rate of criminal corruption between black and white public officials means little to FBI snoops. They relish "nailing" black officials.

For years, blacks have been either excluded from the system all together or given limited access to it; it is little wonder some of them tend to feel justified in "making up" financially for those missed years. Often they are mimicking what they see white officials who held the job before them or hold similar jobs are doing. Black officials have less opportunity to capitalize on their positions since they are not as assiduously courted by "safe" bribe-giving lobbyists as white officials are.

The unremitting pursuit of D.C. Mayor Barry, Tennessee Congressman Ford, and Florida federal Judge Hastings, as well as many other high-ranking blacks, is proof enough of a campaign by federal officials against blacks. The pattern has been too continuing and persistent to charge it off to black paranoia.

While the election of Bill Clinton and the appointment of more fair-minded officials to head up the various branches of the Justice Department and the FBI will hopefully mean an end to such unfair practices, don't bet the farm on it. The rank and file of these organizations are already chafing under new restrictions being placed on them, and will do everything in their power to return to business as usual as soon as possible.

Knowing this, these black officials must learn to live their public and private lives a cut above those of white officials. Blacks are accustomed to being held to a different and higher standard of conduct than whites and shouldn't expect things to change now. They have to, by the way they live and conduct their affairs, make it as difficult as possible for headhunters to make any kind of case on them. Of course it is unfair, but, for most blacks, so is life. This will just put them ahead of the wave of reform, which is surely one day to come. The House banking scandal cost many public officials their jobs, and the mood of the public is, "if they are caught doing wrong, throw them out!"

For too long, most public officials have looked at petty graft and special privileges as the perks of winning an election or working their way up to a high government position. This is no longer acceptable behavior, no matter who is doing it. The fact that I castigate the FBI, whose agents are charged with rooting out such behavior is because that agency, with its history of racism and selective enforcement, certainly isn't in any position to throw stones at any public official. They should clean their own house first, something which will be a long time coming if the past is any indication.

While I can understand from my own experiences with racism how black officials can be tempted into lawbreaking, it doesn't excuse the fact of it. They hold a position of public trust and should conduct themselves accordingly. The truth is, black officials are no more prone to graft and corruption than their white counterparts, which has been far too high for either group. While it is easy to accuse me, a convicted criminal, with being sanctimonious—the pot calling the kettle black—my one saving grace is that I never pretended to be anything other than what I was: a crook.

DRUG CONTROL, NEW YORK STYLE

THE RECENTLY ELECTED Rudolph Giuliani, mayor of "that trash can dream come true" on the bank of the Hudson—New York City—has come into office kicking ass and taking names. Needless to say I, like many other liberals, was more than a bit concerned about his short- and long-range goals, as well as the methods he would employ to achieve them. A fairly conservative Republican and former federal prosecutor, Hizzoner's obvious ambition to one day run for the presidency might cause him to trample on individual and human rights in pursuit of the Grand Prize.

When one of his first moves was to roust the "Squeegee People," those destitute individuals who stand at busy New York intersections washing car windshields, I thought, "Oh boy, white Republican business as usual." While I'm not alone in viewing these walking, talking, begging failures of our economic system with shame and disgrace (society more than the individual doing the begging), to attempt to banish them from our sight and pretend they don't exist is not only meanspirited, but in the long run dangerous. Not providing some alternatives (real alcohol and drug treatment programs would be an excellent start) for these unfortunates is characteristic of what the far-right views of dealing with problems of the underclass consists of—arrest it until it goes away.

More than once while driving in New York, I've risked getting punched in the nose by admonishing a too-aggressive young windowwasher to do something about himself, for Christ's sake! It is indeed frustrating to see young men of color, or old men for that matter, in such dire circumstances. No doubt my reactions on those occasions were unwarranted and in part caused by wounded racial pride; they were making me feel ashamed. All too often they had become so aggressive in their demands for coins they were bordering on "putting the arm" on drivers rather than merely "asking" for a donation for services rendered, especially when the driver happened to be a lone woman.

When the crack epidemic first hit I knew the number of people on the street doing whatever they could for drug money was bound to drastically increase. The risk Mayor Giuliani is running of course is, by forcing these individuals from a fairly innocuous (albeit aggravating) form of panhandling for drug money, these men and women may turn to more serious antisocial behavior of the knife, gun, and baseball bat variety. One thing is for certain: until they receive effective treatment they are going to do *something* to get money for drugs and alcohol. The mayor probably has taken this fact into account but figures these crimes will tend to focus on blacks in neighborhoods other than Manhattan, and therefore are of no great concern.

My view of Mayor Giuliani did, however, undergo a slight revision when he used a sting operation to catch some of New York's Finest committing crimes under color of authority. Everyone in the city has known for years the police routinely shake down drug dealers, taking their drugs (which they put back on the streets by selling to other dealers) and money. Under the previous administration, the local police officers had been instructed to not pay much attention to street drugs sales for fear they would become corrupted by the opportunities for ripoffs and payoffs. They were to leave those crimes to a city-wide antidrug squad. What, in all likelihood, happened was that the local cops told the city-wide squad which dealers to shake down, and no doubt where they lived also. It should be obvious to all that the huge amounts of money involved in the drug trade is enough to corrupt virtually anyone. The arrested police officers are as much victims of our ridiculous drug policies as the crackheads they formerly arrested.

Shaking down drug dealers is a tradition in New York. While I don't want to be viewed as taking up for corrupt police, the average New York City cop has little chance of resisting the temptations of all that cash. It's an occupational hazard. It's not like the young cop new to the drug unit sees an opportunity and takes some money. What happens is the older cops "initiate" the rookie into their secret society. When they make a bust, the money is cut up and the rookie is forced to take a cut. It's either you're down with us or you're against us. And the rookie knows all too well what can happen to some cop who is against them on a drug raid. It's called being killed by "friendly fire." The older cops simply are not going to take a chance on someone informing on them. Everybody is going to be dirty.

In addition to rooting out corruption within the department, the mayor also told the rest of his officers to crack down on street drug dealing. No more waiting for the overworked members of the city-wide drug squad. While this may garner him some immediate positive headlines and get him favorably compared to that crimefighter of another era, Thomas E. Dewey, the chances of his new approach having a long-term effect is virtually nil. All it will mean is the game of drug selling will turn cat and mouse. Like electricity, the drug activity will seek the next path of least resistance.

This is not the thirties. Those methods unfortunately won't work on the drug problem. The mayor, being a Republican, should be able to comprehend the immutability of economics when he is faced with it. *Nothing* will stop the flow of cash and drugs except decriminalization and treatment. The fact that the mayor sprung his police trap so soon makes me somewhat suspicious of his seriousness in addressing corruption within the department. He had to know he could have trapped ten—nay, a 100—times as many officers had he wanted to. Whether he figured the dozen or so arrested officers were enough to send a message to the rest of the force or if he figured that was a sufficient number to grab him some headlines, I guess we'll never know for certain. But one thing is for certain: the cops will be a lot more careful when shaking down drug dealers in the future.

LOSING OUR INNOCENCE
IN CHARLOTTE

IT WAS INEVITABLE if not quite predictable. It eventually had to happen.

As a child of the "first black" generation—as in "the first black to play major league baseball," Jackie Robinson—I've lived to see many "first blacks." Although I can barely remember Jackie Robinson breaking the color barrier, I do remember my baseball fanatic father whooping it up about something. When our Cleveland Indians got its "first black"— Larry Doby—a year or so later, it was more of the same.

Throughout my life I've read with pride of blacks who were the "first" in their chosen field: Althea Gibson, Arthur Ashe, the list could go on and on. I well remember my own family in the mid-sixties being the "first blacks" on our suburban Cleveland street.

Now, however, we have another "first black" we're not so proud of. The "first black" serial killer. Some would argue this dubious distinction should rightly go to Wayne Williams, the Atlanta man convicted of killing twenty-six young boys in Atlanta, but I don't think he fits our cultural criteria of a true serial killer. His clouded and somewhat tainted conviction (which he never confessed to—one of the elements necessary to qualify someone for the category) left blacks who choose to continue to deny a black could become a serial killer ample reason or excuse. Henry Wallace doesn't allow us that luxury.

For years, blacks have taken pride in the fact that our race produced no madmen who methodically killed for the sheer joy of it. We readily understand the rash of homicides committed during the heat of an argument, or some black man eventually running out of his ability to cope with racist taunts, spraying his place of employment with gunfire. We have

110

more trouble dealing with the drive-by shootings which have come to plague our neighborhoods, but we've evidently come to deal with those, too. Killing and death have been the constant companion of our race ever since the dreaded Middle Passage and we've liked to feel our experiences with lynchings, shootings, and brutalizing at the hands of white folks purged our race of the bloodthirsty serial killer. This was something only white folks did. Henry Wallace has forever changed that notion. He has cost the race its innocence.

But even this admitted serial killer's case hasn't escaped the ugly specter of racism. Many of the black civil leaders of Charlotte, North Carolina, have wondered out loud how Wallace could kill ten young women since May of 1992—all of whom lived near (some even worked with) him—and go undetected. Naturally, the local police claim the murders got the same attention any other murders got—at least from them—but people remain unconvinced. And rightly so. It's hard for blacks not to feel that had the young women been white, more would have been done.

Certainly the Fourth Estate would have used its vast powers had the women been white. The Gainesville, Florida, co-ed murders, the Green River killings in Washington State, and the freeway killings of prostitutes in Tennessee and New York States are ample examples of the concern expressed by the media when at least some of the victims are white. Not one word of a killing spree occurring in Charlotte appeared in any national newspaper, or local one for that matter, I suspect.

The sad truth is black lives still don't have the same value as white lives to our criminal-justice system, or the white press for that matter. Who can say how many lives could have been saved had a reporter written a story about the closely connected killings? I don't think some reporter was aware of the connection and just didn't think it newsworthy; I think no reporter, or anyone else in a position of authority in Charlotte, gave a damn about the bodies of young black women turning up at what should have been an alarming rate. It took three victims within four days for them to finally become alarmed. Had the victims been white, the city would have been in a state of siege long before.

The laxity with which black-on-black crime is treated is further high-lighted by the fact that during his killing spree Wallace was twice arrested for rape in the state, once in Allendale and the other time in Rock Hill, only to disappear through the cracks of the criminal-justice system. Can anyone seriously believe this would have happened had his victims been white? A thousand times no!

The road to equality is full of pitfalls and potholes. We as a race have taken pride in the fact that certain crimes rarely occur within our race: child molestation, incest, patricide, and serial killings. These crimes have always been anathema to the black community. However, the Henry Wallace case has forever cost us our innocence.

KEEPING THE PEACE
IN NEW HAVEN

ON JANUARY 9, 1994, *60 Minutes* ran a most enlightening segment on Nick Pastore, the chief of police of New Haven, Connecticut. A career police officer, he had retired from the force in 1981 due to disagreements with enforcement policies of the then chief. He was rehired as chief four years later.

Since taking over the force he has managed to anger and alienate a large percentage of his force. He offered senior officers generous early-retirement packages and transferred one officer who refused the offer to dogcatcher. When other, more-junior officers quit in protest he replaced them with women and minorities, making the department more reflective of the population at large.

He feels, for a number of reasons, women make better police officers than men. They mediate domestic disputes better (a large percentage of police work) and handle victims of sex crimes with more compassion. They are also less inclined to precipitate violent confrontations. This is the crux of the problem he faces with older officers.

The chief's theory of policing is, just as citizens have a family doctor or lawyer, they should also have a family policeman they know well. He has taken officers from behind desks and from behind the wheels of cruisers and put them back on the beat in one-person foot patrols, equipped with beepers so citizens can get in touch with them when necessary.

His old-line officers say they are upset because the chief patrols the neighborhood coffee shops at night looking for loafing officers, but he knows their real gripe is that he expects his officers to treat everyone with respect. Formerly, officers could get all pumped up three or four times a week and go out and kick in some doors and bust some heads but no longer.

The chief, who believes drugs should be decriminalized, stated he had too many white suburbanite officers whose main reason for joining the force was the excitement and thrills the work provided. Black inner-city residents have known this for years. To them, policing is an extension of college contact sports, with the goal being to see how many heads they can bust in one night. Reagan's specious "War" gave them all of the excuses they needed to act out their fantasies as butt-whipping tough guys.

The term "peace officer" is a relic of the past in many police departments since the young, often racist white officers (knowingly hired by police departments) are not seeking to "keep the peace" but are actively seeking out confrontation. They have become part of the problem, rather than the solution. No doubt they have dangerous jobs and occasionally they are going to come up against a suspect who is not going to listen to reason. In those few cases they have to take appropriate action to subdue the suspect with as little danger to themselves as possible. No one should expect them to take needless chances with their safety, but all too often the police overstep their boundaries.

Two long-time members of the New Haven police department, who oppose the chief's new methods, were also interviewed. They had a laundry list of grievances, outstanding among them the complaint that the chief had sent a get-well card to a known gang member/drug dealer who had been in a traffic accident. The chief had gotten to know the man after hearing that the man had vowed to shoot it out with police the next time he was stopped by them. The chief approached the man and had diffused the potentially murderous situation. The chief said he would still send the card to the hospitalized man, knowing how the act would sit with his men. Could it be the officers were upset that they were denied their chance for a shootout?

When officers are trained with an "us versus them" attitude, they actively seek out situations which conform to and justify their training. It's self-fulfilling.

The one question the interviewer Steve Croft didn't ask the two officers (I was dying for him to ask it) was, in light of the fact that the murder, rape, and robbery rates have increased in surrounding communities of similar size but have dropped in New Haven, what is their problem with the chief's methods? Isn't keeping the peace—reducing crime—what it's supposed to be about anyway? Maybe for these officers, and many like them, it isn't.

WHICH SIDE ARE
THE ANGELS ON?

THE CROWD DEMONSTRATING outside the prison was a mixed bunch. While some were against the execution that was about to be carried out, others were in a bloodlust frenzy as they called and hooted for the ultimate retribution. They didn't want John Wayne Gacy to take any additional detours on his road to his final judgment.

The fact that this evil individual had forfeited his right to ever again live freely in society was never the question for anyone, his protestations of innocence aside. However, in my mind, that still could not justify the act that the state was about to perform. Neither does the fact that a majority of Americans is in favor of state-sanctioned killings justify them any better. In the case of capital punishment, the majority is wrong.

In 1954, when the *Brown* v. *Board of Education* decision was handed down by the U.S. Supreme Court, a majority of Americans (overwhelmingly so in the South) didn't agree with school integration. They were wrong. A majority of pre-World War II Germans didn't believe the rights of Jews should be protected. They too were wrong. And using majority public sentiment to justify barbaric behavior is—and always will be—wrong.

Interestingly, the newscaster focused on the fact that members of the Guardian Angels were among the crowd of demonstrators screaming for the act to be carried out, as if their approval of the proceedings somehow added respectability to the planned execution. The fact that these social misfits turned so-called avengers and protectors—who, by and large, are cowards emboldened to become bullies by the power of the mob—still have any credibility left is amazing. The fairly recent admission by the group's founder and leader, Curtis Sliwa, that he staged a number of the incidents where he was supposedly attacked by drug dealers and other ne'er-do-wells should have silenced this group once and for all. The fact that it hasn't is a sad testament to the depths some in our society will sink to in search of heroes.

The brass of the New York police department was 100 percent right when they came out against this organization of young men and women, who will do anything for a little recognition, at its inception. Since these youths are, in the majority, from the crime-infested neighborhoods they were attempting to protect, a responsive chord was immediately struck between them and the story-hungry media. Here were these brave young men and women willing to risk their lives to protect little old ladies making their way home from grocery shopping, the story went. The group's membership took off after the now highly suspect confrontations in which members of the gang "backed down" the bad guys on a New York City subway.

It wasn't long, however, before Sliwa became publicity hungry. The Guardian Angels abandoned the poorer neighborhoods of the South Bronx, Queens, and Brooklyn—where they were known on the street to be a joke and liable to get the cowboy shit kicked out of them—for the glitter of the Great White Way. All of those theatergoers needed protecting from panhandlers much more than low-profile ghetto residents needed protection from muggers.

In short order, the Angels became part of the Broadway scene, parading their scowling selves around in their paramilitary medal-bedecked trademark red berets—shades of brownshirts in the thirties. Soon it was obvious (to the membership if to no one else) that the visitors to the streets near the theater district, which are among the safest and most highly policed in the world, felt more secure with their presence. After the highlifers were safely ensconced in their limos or hotel rooms, the strutting little heroes could always turn their attentions to the backstreets and harass prostitutes and their customers—which they gleefully did.

My point is, the Guardian Angels, in their pompous ignorance and cowardice, typify the death-penalty mentality. Is it any surprise the vast majority of the executions which have been carried out have been done in the overwhelmingly conservative-thinking South? The same South where a black is twenty-seven times as likely to face the supreme penalty for the same crime as a white.

It's high time we dropped all of the hollow, sanctimonious, and specious arguments in support of this heinous activity. The legal costs to the state for a death-penalty case is four to five times what it would cost to house the individual for the rest of his life; the threat of execution does *not* deter crime; it only diminishes and debases our humanity.

Killing even someone as despicable as John Wayne Gacy creates an atmosphere where the death penalty is more acceptable. And as sure as we execute the right person this time, eventually we're going to execute the wrong one, as we have done nearly thirty times in this century, the ones we are aware of. Better to turn the condemned men over to the mob so they can be torn limb from limb than to perfect new oversanitized methods, such as lethal injection. You can't put a humane face on capital punishment—ugly is ugly no matter how well-dressed.

The sad part is that our thirst for blood pulls us down to the same level as the madmen, perverts, and psychopaths from whom we are supposedly protecting ourselves. Society *does* pay a price for its mistakes, if only somewhere down the line.

We are often a foolish and brutish people. We license drivers, dogs, and fishermen—but not gunowners, in spite of the fact that most of our murders are carried out by gunmen. We shouldn't, however, be foolish enough to think death penalties and Guardian Angels will actually do anything to reduce crime and violence in America.

PART
IV

TRAGEDIES AND REMEDIES

THE FOUNDLING

IT'S CHRISTMAS EVE, and for some reason an incident which occurred in my hometown of Cleveland, Ohio, earlier this year is stuck in my mind. A news story concerning the finding of a newborn in a trash bin was the lead item on the evening news. A youngster, who was playing in the vicinity of the trash bin (which was located in the inner-city housing project where he lives), heard the infant's crying and ran home to summon his mother. It wasn't long before the neighborhood was swarming with police, news cameras, and would-be anchorpersons. The television reporters were so anxious for an interview with someone—anyone—I could swear I saw one of them attempting to question a nearby lamppost.

By morning the story was the headline of the local paper and in a hot-off-the-word-processor editorial decrying the incident, the writer wondered who could have done such a heartless thing. Indeed, who could have been responsible for such a mind-boggling act?

With teenage pregnancies at an all-time high, and more common in the ghetto than graduating from high school, there is no longer any social stigma attached to the phenomenon. Maybe it was a teenager who has a parent or grandparent from the old school, who had told the young mother in no uncertain terms, "Don't be bringing no baby home." But if the parent was so concerned about the welfare of the teenager, how could he or she not have noticed the latter stages of the pregnancy?

Or maybe it was a welfare mother stretched to her mental edge, saddled with too large a brood already. Whatever the case, the act in itself was so horrendous, the consensus was soon reached that the mother, whomever she was, had to be temporarily insane.

Then the calls and telegrams began rolling in. Judging from the distant points on the globe where they originated, the story must have made worldwide news. Nothing engenders such an outpouring of genuine human compassion as a foundling. It mattered little that the child was black—it was a baby for God's sake! Some of the offers of adoption no doubt came from individuals who've never seen, or rarely see, a black person in their daily routine, except maybe on television. Incidents such as these somehow transcend human prejudices and bring out the humane compassion which resides in us all.

As the outpouring of concern mounted, the kind of concern which gives hope we can one day all live together in harmony, even the welfare mother whose son found the child staked a touching sort of "finders-keepers" claim to the baby. By the end of the second day, the social-service professionals stepped in and announced the considerable volume of offers would be sifted through and the one which best suited the interests of the child would be selected. No doubt the couple chosen to receive the baby would be stable, middle-class, and able to offer the newborn every conceivable benefit: decent suburban housing, a safe and secure environment, and excellent educational opportunities. All of the ingredients a newborn needs to start off on the right foot in life. This is the way the story should end.

But what if the mother had kept the child? Or had put it up for adoption through the regular process where it would have been in competition with thousands of other less-favored black children? Of course the child's future wouldn't have been so bright then, for it either would have been placed in foster home after foster home, shuttled about for most of its young life like a piece of lost mail, or would have had to take its chances in a ghetto housing project along with millions of other black children. And the chances of children in these circumstances reaching maturity are becoming slimmer all the time. Those who do survive the mean streets stand a better than 50 percent chance of going to prison before they reach their majority.

So it seems the mother unknowingly did the right thing after all. Now at least her offspring will, due to the widespread publicity generated by the incident, end up with a caring and loving family which will provide all of the advantages every child needs to flourish and deserves. But the shame of the incident is that the best thing for black babies born into our nation's ghettos with no futures, hopes, or prospects is to be thrown into a trash bin. Merry Christmas.

THE TRUTH ABOUT
TEEN PREGNANCIES

AN ARTICLE in the February 22, 1994, issue of *USA Today* entitled "Teen Births 'Formula for Disaster'" tracks the problematic rise in the teenage-mother birthrate—mainly of the underclass—in the last two decades.

Since the phenomenon is the engine which drives the twin runaway trains of poverty and violent crime in our country, it is the most singularly important social issue in America today. There is no denying where tomorrow's poor and criminals will come from: our nation's ghettos, and they will in all likelihood be the offspring of a teenager.

However, the article, which should encourage much-needed debate on the subject, missed the mark entirely in addressing one facet of the issue. It stated that "academic surveys repeatedly find that three-fourths of teenagers don't plan their pregnancies." That this disingenuous information which the young mothers supply to the surveyors is taken at face value is a testament to the latter's gullibility.

What did they expect the teenagers to answer? These young mothers, who are now in their "martyr" stage (making every sacrifice for their helpless child) aren't about to forfeit all of the sympathy, assistance, and benefits they are currently receiving for their "mistake" by admitting it wasn't a mistake after all. While society has changed to the point where teenage pregnancies don't carry the social stigma they once did, it still hasn't reached the point where these children can comfortably admit they got pregnant on purpose. In fact, I don't doubt most of them have told themselves they didn't want to become pregnant as they neglected to use birth control. They've told the lie to themselves so often and for so long they now believe it themselves. But for us to formulate a policy to reduce these births based on these obvious untruths is foolhardy.

An excellent parallel can be found in prison, where the majority of the fathers of these teenage women's babies resides. Many young men repeatedly return to prison again and again, leading many observers, myself included, to conclude they have become institutionalized and actually prefer to be in a setting where they know what tomorrow will bring over being at liberty, with all of its attendant worries and fears. Yet, if these young men were ever asked if they indeed do prefer prison, the answer will be a resounding "no!", with maybe a punch thrown in the direction of the questioner's nose for even daring to make such an assumption. They, like the young women who are having the babies at such tender ages, simply can't tell the truth—not even to themselves. Even in their world this kind of behavior can't be admitted to. It *had* to be an accident or circumstances beyond their control.

If these births aren't planned then we have to look elsewhere for answers. Three options immediately come to mind: the first, and the one in vogue at present, is these births are the result of a lack of sex education, coupled with restricted access to birth-control devices. I find this hard to believe since, while condoms aren't exactly a dime a dozen, they are fast approaching this price. In most inner cities, one can readily find clinics which will pay you the dime to take them.

I sincerely wish this were the cause of the problem for then we'd soon be able to solve it. However, I strongly suspect something more ominous than a lack of information is truly the culprit. The process of procreation isn't really all that complicated, not even for thirteen year olds. Certainly additional sex education wouldn't hurt, but don't look for it to reduce the teen birthrate. In fact, it is somewhat racist to suggest these girls of the underclass are so dumb they can't avoid getting pregnant even when they don't want to, but that concept nicely fits some people's prejudices. Even in the face of the now-murderous antiabortion forces (which are only concerned with unwanted children being born and make no efforts to insure the care of these children for the next eighteen or twenty years) we can provide access to education and birth-control devices. But, as I formerly said, don't expect this to impact on the problem very much.

The second premise is pretty ridiculous but no doubt still holds some validity in some minds. This is the whispered theory that minorities are just more fertile. This really doesn't deserve refuting but must be kept in mind when looking at a problem with such far-reaching social consequences.

The last premise, however, while just as racist as the previous one, does have to be addressed. It is the specious logic that since girls of the under-class have more babies at an early age they must simply be more promiscuous than their white counterparts. The irony is that quite the opposite is closer to the truth. Minority teenagers probably engage in less sex than white ones.

The reason is simple. The sexual revolution pretty much passed the minority community by. Minority girls are not as comfortable with their sexuality as white girls. And my very unscientific opinion is that other than to become pregnant minority teenagers (except for the few wild ones) are not generally promiscuous. But this myth too easily fits the racists' views and prevents us from making an accurate assessment of the problem.

One factor which isn't considered is the whispered rumor which circulates in our nation's ghettos. It holds that whites are secretly engaged in a program of genocide against the black race. The fact that so many black men of child-producing age are incarcerated for crimes for which only they go to prison gives a measure of validity to this theory. For teenage girls who can foresee only a reproductive not productive future, what better service for their people can they perform—according to their twisted but understandable logic—than to propagate their own race? But at what cost to themselves, to their children, and to us all?

Rethinking Our Solutions to Teen Pregnancies

Before an adequate solution to a problem can be formulated it first must be accurately assessed and understood. Both Dr. Joycelyn Elders and Janet Reno are correct when they state the greatest problem facing the underclass—and the root cause of most poverty, crime, and violence in our country—is teen pregnancies. Babies having babies. This phenomenon is putting a large portion of the black race at peril.

However, because of a lack of understanding of the causes of this pernicious problem, these two otherwise bright women, who to a large degree determine how our resources will be deployed in this area, are about to propose solutions which will not and cannot work. And if history is any precedent, the victims of ill-conceived government programs will again be blamed for their failure.

By all indications, they intend to attack the problem with additional sex and family-planning education and the wider use of condoms. These methods presuppose the causes of these pregnancies are either a lack of information or improper use of birth control; unfortunately neither is the case. The vast majority of these pregnancies are planned.

Anaïs Nin, the brilliant feminist author wrote that "we must see things as they are, not as we are." The mistake these two well-meaning women are making is visualizing the problem through their own eyes and value systems, not through the eyes of the teenagers who are having babies. What someone of the middle-class views as failure, these girls of the underclass see as success. Take a look at the situation from the girls' points of view: most of them, having been raised on welfare, have no concept of a future which offers a career. The only promise America holds for them is an opportunity to flip hamburgers or fill some other minimum-wage job. All adolescents wish desperately to become adults, an important part of the maturing process. However, while young women raised with a sense of a future are willing to forestall engaging in conduct which might inhibit their career plans, these children of the underclass don't have, in their minds, any future to protect. For these girls, success is growing up as fast as possible, and the fastest method they know is to have a baby. The benefits, for them, are too obvious: they become emancipated minors who now, maybe for the first time in their lives, have something all their own to love and need them. They get, as proof of their adulthood, their very own welfare check (and probably one for the newborn), and they garner all of the attention and special care expectant and new mothers everywhere traditionally receive (since any "shame" associated with unwed pregnancies without benefit of marriage has long ago been relegated to the trash heap of "outdated" morality). The incentive for them to become pregnant is simply too overwhelming. And we will not be able to "educate" them out of their beliefs in the short term.

What are we to do? If we are to ever solve the problems of the under class we must come to grips with this phenomenon. The more hardhearted social scientists suggest we simply break the social contract we have conditioned these young girls to come to expect to be fulfilled and cut off all funding for their newborns. Let them starve. Of course, the real solution is to provide these girls with futures they don't want to jeopardize by becoming pregnant, but this takes time.

The only workable solution—in the short term—is to use recently closed military bases for Children's Camps. Safe places young women where upon becoming pregnant can go to give birth to healthy babies, and to remain there for the first three years of the child's life while middle-class black and other minority volunteers can assist these girls in inculcating their offspring with the values they will need to possess to become productive members of society.

At present we expect these girls to take their newborns back to the same ghettos which failed them and raise something other than failures. This, in the vast majority of cases, can't be done. Newborn males condemned to being raised in ghetto conditions may just as well be given a prison number at birth, so great is the possibility they will eventually need it. Female babies should be assigned their permanent welfare identification numbers. No amount of outreach or head-start programs can overcome the negative influences of being raised in an environment where the child will, before his third birthday, pick up a discarded crack pipe and ask, "Mommy, what is this?"

Society already pays for all of the expenses of these mothers and their children, so cost can't be used as an excuse. Doesn't it just make sense to deliver these services in a setting where society has better control of the outcome of these newborns' and their still-growing mothers' lives?

CHILDFARE

THOUGH INNATELY INTELLIGENT and quite ambitious otherwise, a young man I was tutoring in a GED class was disdainful of the whole process of formal education. It wasn't that he was having trouble handling the material, he wasn't; he just couldn't visualize the need for additional formal education. He felt the knowledge I was attempting to impart had little practical value for him, now or in the future. Many other young blacks have become similarly disenchanted with education due to racism, both real and perceived. They have the attitude that they'll never get a fair opportunity anyway, so why bother? It's their way of rebelling against something they feel powerless against. I had to reach down deep to come up with an adequate answer.

I questioned the young man about his plans for earning a living upon his release and he confidently replied his future was set: he was going to make it big shooting music videos. When I attempted to tie the need for additional education to his dream he assured me he already knew all there was to operating a home video camera!

From previous conversations with the dude, I knew he was an auto-racing buff. I attempted to use that field to construct a useful analogy. "Suppose a driver showed up at the Indy 500 and wanted to enter his straight-off-the-assembly-line auto, he'd be laughed off the track, right?" The young man readily agreed. "Well that's the reception you're going to get if you show up somewhere with a home video camera saying you want to make music videos. It's a bit more complicated than that. Why don't you try to get some information about the types of equipment currently being used in the field?"

I felt quite proud of myself as I walked away. Unfortunately, I later found out I had no impact whatsoever on the young man. So many young blacks don't have the faintest notion of what it takes to have an opportunity for success in the real world. In fact, many of them have such low goals they think obtaining a GED is the end of the education process instead of the very beginning.

And these youths are passing their limited views and ambitions on the next generation of ghetto children. In the last essay, I called for the establishment of Children's Camps where young girls would go to receive proper prenatal care and to remain with their child for the first three or four years of the child's life. While I still feel taking the mother and child out of the ghetto is by far the best way to insure an adequate upbringing for the newborn, I have to be realistic about the willingness of society to make the necessary commitment to such a program. Since half a loaf is better than none, I submit that if the camps proved too much of an undertaking (they really shouldn't), then we should institute other methods of dealing with the growing problem of babies raising babies.

Many states are implementing "Workfare" programs which require welfare mothers to work in order to receive benefits. We should institute "Childfare," which would require expectant mothers to receive proper prenatal care and to attend childcare classes both before and after giving birth. We can even offer small financial incentives to accomplish this and dis-incentives (such as the termination of welfare payments) for those who don't get with the program.

Currently we trust too much in the good intentions of these young mothers to provide their offspring with adequate care, and far too often the newborns have been left wanting. It's not that the vast majority of the mothers don't do the best they know how to do; they do. It's just their best is proving to be not good enough. Witness the rising crime rates.

Many of these—young women, many of whom are really girls—come from homes where little premium is placed on education. In many of them, books and other educational materials are a rarity. I am not faulting these girls, they simply don't know any better. But we do and I find nothing obnoxious about compelling them to provide their children with what we know is necessary for the child to have at least a decent shot in the world.

I personally feel every mother who wishes to stay home with her newborn should be allowed to do so without incurring financial hardship, at least for the first two years. Some middle-class mothers do manage to juggle motherhood and career but they are better prepared for the tasks, and have better support systems. The mothers of the underclass need to concentrate solely on the proper raising of their children during this period for if they fail to do an adequate job, society will be the one to pay for their failure in increased crime and violence later on down the line.

Of course these young mothers should be provided with an opportunity to continue with their own education during this period. There is an excellent program in Brooklyn, New York, where young mothers attend college classes while their children are in classes right down the hall. The results of this program indicate it should be expanded to high-school grades also.

Head-start programs were instituted because it became evident that we were waiting too long before beginning a child's formal education. I think we can now safely say education begins in the womb, right after conception. We shouldn't wait until some arbitrary date in the future to begin the education process.

Until we can somehow convince these girls to wait before embarking on parenthood we had better be prepared at least to assist them in raising the child properly. Or be prepared for another generation of failures, with all of the attendant crime and violence.

THE COMING MENACE

As bad as conditions are in many of our nation's ravaged inner-city neighborhoods, in approximately three to five years they are going to get worse, a lot worse. And not just the gradual, incremental deterioration witnessed in the last three decades, but a sharp, large-scale, cataclysmic decline, with all of the attendant by-products of increased crime and violence.

For then the first generation of children born during the crack era will be coming of age, old enough to be roaming the streets of our cities, creating havoc. And these youngsters, the first to never know a time when crack didn't exist, promise to be monsters, due to the neglect they've suffered at the hands of crack-addicted parents and the possibility of genetic damage due to drugs in the womb.

The problems of the ghettos—crime, violence, child neglect, abuse, despair, and poverty—have been with us for centuries, producing generation after generation of societal predators. But the relatively recent crack phenomenon will cause a quantum leap backwards and downwards in our society if something isn't done. Never before in history have so many children been so neglected and brutalized as when crack came into widespread use in the eighties.

Before a group of Columbia University graduate chemistry students (allegedly, but with good evidence) developed a method of "freeing up the base" of cocaine and started smoking it, the drug was considered, while somewhat dangerous, very chic in many quarters. Rock stars, high-powered executives (both in government and private sectors), movie actors, and criminals of every stripe thought it fashionable to do a few lines every now and then. In the major media centers of New York, Miami, and Los Angeles few "gentlemen" dared to go courting a slick young woman without a gram or two of the devil's dandruff. It was as commonplace as taking flowers or a good bottle of wine in bygone eras.

Sure, occasionally someone might get strung out on snorting cocaine, but rarely—their contemporaries would treat them with the same disdain reserved for someone who had become addicted to champagne—it just wasn't cool. Back then, while cocaine was not unknown in the ghettos, it wasn't extremely popular due to its high cost. A little weed and wine, with an occasional toot of something, had to suffice. Crack changed all of that.

When the Beautiful People first tried crack it was hailed by the drug culture as a unique breakthrough in blowing one's mind. It quickly became the rage as people reached new levels of brain-scrambling "flashes of insight" never before experienced by mere snorting. Then it happened; someone attempted to quit and found he couldn't. The same people who for years had snorted cocaine on and off without any problem and felt they could take it or leave it found leaving crack difficult, if not impossible. While formerly they had spent a portion of their discretionary incomes on weekend cocaine, they now found themselves making mad midnight dashes to bank teller machines until all of their money was gone.

When crack reached the masses in the ghettos it became, and has remained, a full-fledged epidemic. Ghetto parents and welfare mothers, wanting to try this "new thing" for themselves soon found out what wealthier users already knew: one hit is too many and a million ain't enough. Since their poverty denied them the socially acceptable methods of seeking thrills (something which is innate in humans), such as bungee jumping, skiing, motorcycle racing, hang gliding, and the like, they were stuck with seeking thrills at ten dollars a hit.

Seemingly no parent in his right mind would abandon his offspring for days on end while he pursued another "bump," but then crack smokers aren't in their right minds. The addiction is that strong. Soon a new creature appeared in doorways and alleys of the mean streets: the now ubiquitous "strawberry." Women (often mere girls) so addicted they will literally do *anything* for another blast. And now these poor addicted souls' children are coming of age. They will soon be able to wield knives, clubs, and guns. Woe be unto us.

If something—a joint effort between citizens and the government—isn't done, and done soon, the damage is going to be more terrible than anything we've experienced thus far. I shudder with fear.

THE BORDER

ANOTHER REASON AMERICA WILL never be able to win the so-called War on Drugs has to do with what I'll call "The Economics of the Foot Soldier Factor." It goes like this:

Formerly the majority of cocaine which came into the United States came in by the efforts of professional smugglers via private planes and boats. Only amateurs brought in small amounts on their persons or in their luggage. That method, except for maybe some heroin brought in via "mules," was the stuff of Hollywood fiction, until fairly recently.

When the feds cracked down on the small planes making drops or landings all over the southeastern United States, and made similar efforts to interdict the cocaine and marijuana from being brought in by commercial and pleasure boats, the smugglers had to find another method of getting their product to market.

Since all interdiction is basically just a game of high-stakes cat and mouse played out between the DEA and the smugglers, the federal officials probably knew before the smugglers did where they would go next. One thing was for sure: the game would continue. For it to stop would violate one of the rock-solid, immutable principles on which our system of free enterprise is founded: supply and demand. Any high-school student should be able to tell you roughly how it works: the price for any commodity will rise in direct proportion to its scarcity. And it will continue to rise until the demand, at some price, is met. In other words all the War on Drugs can hope to accomplish is to raise the price of a kilo, something the drug smugglers at the top of the heap certainly don't mind. What they would mind is if we finally got smart and legalized the crap. The bottom would fall out of the prices.

Someone will always be willing to run the risk of bringing the cocaine into the country if the price is right, and if interdiction efforts ever proved successful the prices would again rise to the $50,000 per kilo, the prices of twenty years ago. For cocaine not to follow the same laws of economics as any other commodity is impossible. It has to, and despite our government's best efforts at interdiction, the prices have fallen since the War on Drugs began in the eighties.

The smugglers pretty much abandoned the large plane-load shipment strategy and instead concentrated on the "swarm" technique, the foot soldiers I wrote of. Every day, literally thousands of Mexicans and Central and South Americans are massed at the border just below the Rio Grande waiting for nightfall. Many are waiting to make a dash to a better life, but some, simply by making the dash almost instantly achieve a better life. These are the aliens who are carrying backpacks filled with cocaine.

As they make their assault on the border, the agents have a tough time knowing which aliens are carrying drugs and which are simply seeking work. If they get too close to one of the "mules" the backpack is shucked while leading the agents on a merry chase over the inhospitable terrain and may be picked up by another alien making the crossing. If the agent catches the "mule" with the backpack, he is taking a drop out of an overflowing bucket. The kilos, which sell for between 10,000 and 20,000 dollars on this side of the border costs the smugglers only one-tenth of what they sell it for. Believe me, they have tons and tons of it ready for market.

Now what happens to the poor "mule" who got caught with the backpack? If he had successfully delivered his load he would have received 1,000 dollars, the average yearly income of the area he originates from. Not bad for one night's work. If he's caught the poor guy will go to federal prison. You may feel badly for him or his family, who probably needed the money desperately, but consider this: he will go to a prison which has a factory run by a Department of Justice company known as Unicor.

Unicor runs factories in virtually all American federal prisons and makes everything from glue brushes to wire cable used in the defense industry to furniture. If you've ever taken a seat in an IRS office you were probably sitting on prison-made furniture. The rate of pay isn't that great by American standards, only fifty cents to somewhere around two bucks an hour. But to our friend who got caught with the backpack full of cocaine this is like heaven. He can make up to 4,000 dollars a year, of which he can send every penny home to his family if he so chooses.

Of course, federal laws forbid his being hired at Unicor but according to a Unicor lawyer (*Time* magazine, March, 1994) the law is never enforced.

I'm not trying to knock this guy out of his job at Unicor—far from it. I'm merely pointing out why we'll never be able to stem the tide of drugs coming across our southern border.

A good analogy is imagining someone offering an American to take some drugs to Canada. If he makes it safely across the border (the chances are a thousand to one he will) he'll get paid his average yearly income, provided of course he had a job. But still the average income is, let's figure low, 20,000 to 25,000. That's what the American would get if he's successful. If he's caught, the Canadian government will put him in prison and give him a job where he can make three to four times that to send home. I wonder how many Americans would take a chance on a deal like that? They would probably be massed at the Canadian border. Just like they are in Mexico.

THE WAR WE CAN'T WIN

THE FORMER ATTORNEY GENERAL for the country of Colombia, Gustavo de Greiff, recently stated on *60 Minutes* that if America can't reduce the demand for cocaine it matters little how many drug lords his country locks up.

This statement is from the one individual in the world most responsible for controlling the flow of cocaine from South America to our country. While some may say this is a wimpish way to address the problem, one has only to realize that this man of advanced years who could reasonably expect to live out his life in relative tranquility, has taken one of the most dangerous jobs in the world to prove that notion wrong.

In recent years more than 350 judges, prosecutors, and police officials have been killed in Colombia by the drug cartels. The situation is so bad Mr. de Greiff instituted a method whereby accused criminals no longer see the face of the prosecutors, or the judges for that matter. But in a country where bribes are still very effective, and the cocaine cartels have more money than the government, it doesn't take much for the criminals to find out the names of the prosecutors, and to threaten them and their families.

In this country last year we spent 25 billion dollars in an attempt to control a 100-billion-dollar cocaine industry without much success. And as much as no one wants to admit defeat in the War on Drugs, it is time to at least reconsider it.

Some laws are immutable, and the economic law of supply and demand is one of those. If there is a demand, there *will* be a supply. Period.

All of our efforts to dry up the supply will avail little other than slightly raising the price of drugs. No matter how many people are arrested, no matter how harsh the sentences for violating the laws, someone will, considering the vast amounts of money involved, take the risks.

When the penalties are increased, perhaps those involved in the trade, not wishing to pay the stiffer price, might be disinclined to continue with the enterprises. However, new, younger men coming into the trade care less about the stiffer penalties since they can't remember the time when they were lower.

Often our near fanatical stance against drugs and their usage rings hollow. Especially in light of the fact that alcohol and tobacco are drugs which cause many more problems in terms of sickness, accidents, broken families, and lost time from work. Most people don't like to admit their biggest opposition to drugs stems from the fact that they simply hate to see young, mostly black men driving around in $50,000 cars while they are struggling to make payments on the family station wagon.

But is jealousy enough to push ourselves to the brink of bankruptcy? For, if the next decade sees the increase the last one has, eventually we'll be headed in that direction, for no nation can keep doubling its prison population every ten years and remain healthy, financially or otherwise.

And if our nation's police officers enforced the laws equally on everyone, the rate of incarceration would rise even much faster. The fact that unequal justice is making a mockery of our criminal court system is all the more reason to reconsider present laws. With all of the concern over rising crime rates our sanctions against most drugs is akin to shooting ourselves in the foot. If marijuana and then cocaine were decriminalized and taxed, the first direct benefit would be a sudden drop in the number of young men killed in the streets of our ghettos. With the drugs no longer illegal the prices would drop dramatically, making them not worth killing or losing one's life over. There would also be a decline in the number of youths visiting Mercedes dealers with bags of cash.

By regulating and taxing the now-illegal substances they would then produce an income instead of an outflow. Other countries have already taken this sensible approach with no discernible decline in the quality of life of its citizenry.

While in the short run, the amount of users no doubt will rise, once the attractiveness of using a substance which is against the law disappears the numbers will soon decline. This was our experience immediately following Prohibition, and if society didn't react in the same manner our legislators could quickly reinstitute the laws against so-called dangerous drugs.

Since it is impossible to solve a medical, economic, and social problem with legal methods, eventually we'll have to try decriminalization, at least for a trial period of five years. The only question is how many billions of dollars poorer will we be before doing so?

INTERDICTION AND ADDICTION

THE VIRTUALLY SIMULTANEOUS DEATHS of two youth culture icons—River Phoenix and Kurt Cobain—due to heroin abuse, coupled with a rise in heroin-related emergency room visits, both herald another new drug epidemic, according to the officials at the Drug Enforcement Administration.

DEA officials are using the hospital-gleaned statistics in conjunction with the presence of a purer quality of heroin they've recently seized to tout heroin as the "drug most likely to be abused in the coming year." The truth is, these officials don't know if the increase in emergency room visits is due to an increase in the number of abusers or if it can be attributed to the same amount of users failing to take into account the purer quality of the drug, and thus overdosing. Either scenario is indeed a sad commentary. But it doesn't excuse what the DEA is doing with the issue.

Every year DEA officials come up with a new drug "panic." Last year it was "ice," if my memory serves me correctly. Ice is a new, smokable form of methamphetamine from Hawaii that was supposed to take the mainland by storm and lay it low. The year before was MDA, whatever the hell that is. The year before that it was ecstasy which was supposed to be the new menace. Who knows what it will be next year. None of the previous "phantom epidemics" which were so direly predicted by the DEA materialized, I might add.

Our country's drug problem is certainly serious enough without these Chicken Littles of the DEA scaring the bejeebers out of the body politic every year by predicting the sky is falling merely to increase the amount Congress allots its agency. If you look back over the last four yearly "panics" you'll discover that all of the DEA's predictions were made during the same month, right before Congress exercises its budgetary largess.

The DEA is afraid that our political leaders will one day wise up and begin allocating the lion's share of the money where it will do some good—in treatment and rehabilitation—if they don't continue to blow smoke in the Congresspersons' faces. Where, oh where, would that leave these drugstore cowboys? Without money for horse or hay.

Another truth is that the DEA—and virtually every other drug interdiction organization in any country on the face of the earth—is cost "ineffective." They simply cannot control the flow of illegal drugs; it can't be done no matter how much money is spent in the effort.

Without having a snitch supply it with information, the DEA couldn't find its rear with both hands. The draconian drug sentences being meted out under federal mandatory minimum guidelines are causing brother to inform on brother. While federal prosecutors laugh up their collective sleeves at this fairly recent turn of events, they are indeed being shortsighted.

No country will remain a stable, freedom-loving democracy when turned by federal police into a nation of quislings. It's one thing to be an upstanding citizen and inform the police of, say, a violent or property crime; we all have our duties as members of this society. It's quite another when family members and friends are forced to roll over on each other under threat of being locked up, virtually for life. This turning brother against brother, father against son, wife against husband, and friend against friend may seem like effective law enforcement for the nonce, and judging by the resultant rising prison population rates it certainly is. But the insidious, unseen, and uncalculated damage done to the very fabric and spirit of our society by tearing relationships—yes, even the "criminal" ones of drug traffickers—asunder, making neighbor suspicious of neighbor, all in the name of a specious War on Drugs will one day present us with a moral bill we are going to be unwilling, or unable, to pay. We are, with our insane drug policies, throwing the baby out with the bathwater.

If there is indeed an increase in heroin use among middle-class whites it has more to do with the zeitgeist than with some nefarious anti-American plot schemed up by some fiendish druglord half a world away. If young white kids (if the suspected or predicted increase in usage was confined to minority youth, I can assure you there would be no "panic"; it would be a nonissue) in increasing numbers are "chasing the dragon," it is due to the feeling of hopelessness and nihilism which pervades their culture, not due to someone pushing drugs on them. Availability doesn't drive demand, it's the other way around. These excuses for any increase in drug usage among those who are supposed to know better are a thinly disguised attempt to place the blame of our failing social policies (which is what has created "Generation X") on some distant bogeyman.

If these youths are in fact seeking to escape into the rose-colored world of sensation-numbing heroin in increasing numbers, then it is due to their disillusionment with the world their parents have created and now wish to will to them. By neglecting these, their children—the ground they walk on, the air they breathe, and the water they drink while in constant hot pursuit of the almighty dollar—they have left their offspring without the moral underpinnings or desire to resist temptation.

Being the first generation to have to reduce its sights—to not be able to expect life to be better for them than it was for their parents—is a lot for today's youth to have to handle. They have inherited a world sullied by pollution, beset by AIDS, and delineated by an ongoing argument among millionaire Senators as to whether or not we can afford to provide basic health care for all of our citizens. Is it any wonder young people are seeking an escape? And increased DEA budgets rob them of the opportunity for much-needed treatment. But, yet and still, heroin will not provide the answers.

If they are beginning to play around with heroin they had better be damn careful. This is not the same thing as the "mothers' little helpers" they probably grew up watching their parents wash down with booze. This is an *extremely* dangerous and addictive drug. Waking up every morning having to "get straight" within the hour or pay the excruciating price of severe cramps, chills, and fever isn't at all glamorous, no matter which superstar is supposedly using it. In fact, when you've seen it up close, it's downright disgusting.

FIGHTING THAT GIANT

IT IS SOMEWHAT IRONIC that two of the most pernicious plagues to ever afflict mankind—AIDS and crack—both made their initial appearance at roughly the same time, in the early eighties.

While AIDS will eventually be cured by trained scientists, crack addiction can only be successfully combatted not by trained social scientists alone, but also by former addicts, such as myself.

The heroin epidemic of the late fifties and early sixties proved fairly resistant to the best efforts of drug counselors and it wasn't until a group of ex-addicts started Daytop Village, a drug-treatment program in New York, and Syanon, in California, that we were able to develop strategies which eventually proved successful. Alcoholics Anonymous—started by former alcoholics—had much the same effect on alcoholism in the thirties.

I don't know if those two groups produced any jealousy among trained professional with their success, but in the field of crack addiction there seems to be a reluctance on the part of professionals to include ex-addicts in the development of treatment modalities. I can't help but wonder if this is because many of those addicted to crack are black.

However, for reasons I won't detail here due to constraints of time and space, ex-crack abusers should be the first people with whom someone attempting to kick the crack habit should come into contact. I have no problem with graduate-school-educated, trained professionals intervening later to assist the person in mastering strategies to avoid relapse into drug use. There is a necessary function for these people to fulfill, but not at the beginning. At that point they should only supervise the directly intervening former abusers.

The proof of the failure of the professionals' methods lies in the numbers: only 10 percent of crack addicts who go through treatment remain clean two years later. Since crack has been around less than twenty years, it is little wonder we have yet to solve the riddle of its addiction. These things take time. However, the mistake the professionals made from the onset was to take a heroin or alcohol treatment program, put new wheels on it, and attempt to use it to treat crack addiction. Their mistake is excusable in light of the fact they had nothing else to try. While all addictions have some basic things in common, the methods of treatment have to take into account their differences also.

One of the reasons drug counselors have trouble connecting with crack abusers is the "embarrassment factor." It's just easier to swap old war stories about the drug with someone who himself has fought the wars. People do some things while chasing crack they are very ashamed of later.

An alcoholic or heroin addict can "get straight" for ten to twenty dollars, the cost of a fifth of booze or a bag of smack. They can then gratefully return to oblivion, at least for a number of hours. Not so the crack addict. Once they take one five-dollar hit, within fifteen minutes they will do *anything,* I repeat, *anything* for another. And, God help them, most of them have.

It is not easy to talk to someone about this who has not been through these kinds of experiences also because of the "embarrassment factor." Until the person can talk honestly about it, treatment can't begin. No one wants to risk the censure of others, no matter how trained the specialist.

When a person is first denied access to crack she will begin to have vivid dreams about getting high. Flashbacks. These continue for approximately six months and then slack off. Until this occurs, it does a drug counselor little good to attempt treatment. The person might sit there and mouth all of the right answers but in the back of her mind she is still attempting to figure out how she will beat the crack monster on her next encounter. She doesn't even begin to rule out the possibility of trying it "one more time" until after she stops dreaming about it.

Any serious crack-intervention program must begin with a minimum of six months completely away from the drug. Then counseling can come into play. Therein is the crux of the problem: how do you keep a crack addict away from it for six months? There's only way I know of, lock him up. This is not intended to be punitive, it's just that nothing else will work. Period. It takes one to know one.

REAL STRAIGHT TALK
ABOUT DRUGS

A RECENT *WASHINGTON POST* EDITORIAL (weekly edition, December 20 to 27, 1993) argues against even considering exploring the consequences of decriminalizing drugs in typical knee-jerk fashion. Responses of this type, regardless of subject matter, first require that any logic and reason be thrown out the window. And since drugs have become such an ominous presence in American life any attempt at rational debate is doomed by the media from the beginning.

Dr. Joycelyn Elders, the former U.S. Surgeon General, touched off a firestorm of controversy a few days before the editorial was written by casually remarking to a news reporter at a conference she was attending that decriminalization of drugs ought to at least be explored. She stated that other countries that have taken the step of legalizing drugs have experienced a reduction in crime with no increase in the rate of drug use.

The *Post* editorial faulted her for not citing specific examples in her off-the-cuff observations and stated "experts" disagree with her on that point. While the *Post* didn't cite its "experts" by name, the sorry state of affairs America finds itself vis-à-vis drugs causes me to be extremely suspect of the skills of anyone in America who passes himself off as a "drug expert." By definition, an "expert" is someone who possesses enough knowledge in a given field to bring her expertise to bear on the particular problems of said field. I don't see anyone in America bringing any expertise to bear in the field of illegal drugs. Could the "experts" cited by the *Post* be the progeny of those brilliant government filmmakers of the twenties who gave us the movie *Reefer Madness*?

The *Post* editorial hearkened all the way back to near the beginning of the century when the Harrison Act, which outlawed dangerous drugs, was first passed. The *Post* stated that at the time "drugs caused tremendous health and social problems at every level of society." Has making them illegal solved, or even lessened, those problems? No. No more than Prohibition had a ghost of a chance of solving the problems of alcoholism. Health and social problems can never be solved with legal means.

Will legalization, as the *Post* editorial concluded, lead to more problems than it would solve? Our only national experience in this area is with the Volstead Act, and those experiences suggest otherwise. Once Prohibition was repealed, alcohol lost some of its attraction for many people who were drinking simply *because* it was against the law. People didn't want to feel the government could tell them what to do in this area of their lives, and as soon as Prohibition was repealed drinking declined, not increasing as the doomsayers predicted. A similar phenomenon probably would occur with the legalization of drugs.

But, in truth, we won't know what might happen if we took such a fateful step, except a sharp decline in the number of drug-related killings. If, say, after a five year trial period we weren't experiencing the desired results, we could just as easily reinstitute new, tougher drug laws. As the situation now stands, we risk little by making the attempt since things could scarcely get worse than they are at present.

The *Post* editorial reasoned that without drug laws more people would tend toward using illicit substances. This statement demonstrates an amazing lack of understanding of the drug culture, or human nature for that matter. No one avoids drug use simply because drugs are illegal. If the laws against them were effective, we wouldn't have constantly rising prison population rates. We can't legislate ourselves out of the problem.

Next the editorial attempts to demagogue the issue by using scare tactics. It suggests that without laws against drugs the motor vehicle accident rates would skyrocket, as would spousal abuse. Shame on them. They know, or should know, nothing anyone takes into their bodies has near the propensity to cause either of the two problems they mentioned as well as alcohol. Not that we need to legalize other substances which cause people to break the social contract, but they know most of the violence which is associated with drugs stems from someone attempting to get the money for them, not after their use. And as for driving, nothing makes a driver overcompensate as much as drug use. Only alcohol causes drivers to throw caution to the wind with reckless abandon.

Legalization would spur the research which would quickly lead to the creation of new designer drugs which had few, if any, negative side effects. The fact is, our Judeo-Christian ethics are dead set against any drug, other than alcohol, which produces euphoria, no matter how innocuous the drug might be. We stopped the baiting of bears in this country many years ago, not because of the harm it was doing to the bears, but because of the pleasure it was providing for the baiters.

Because our forefathers made a mistake ninety years ago when they, by passing the Harrison Act, began treating a medical problem with legal means doesn't mean we should continue down this blind alley. A large part of our present problem is that we have allowed politicians to demonize drugs simply to use them as a vehicle to ride to reelection. This virtually guarantees that they cut off any intelligent debate on the issue. Political fortunes are involved here, the truth be damned. When Americans declare war on someone or something, they don't like to lose. However, this is not only a war we can't win, it's one which shouldn't have even been fought, at least not with the weapons we've so far chosen.

I've never wished for harm to come to another human being, but until young whites are being mowed down in the streets over drug profits and turf as black and Latino youths currently are, there will be no national debate on legalizing drugs.

The Cure for Crack Addiction

"MAY THE MOST you wish for be the least you get," goes the proverb. And it's certainly true in regards to drug abuse treatment. In conjunction with my desire to see the United States come up with a sane and workable legal strategy concerning drugs (decriminalization), I hoped something positive would be done in the vital area of drug treatment. Crack treatment, to be more specific, since this is the drug which is giving us the most problems at present and the one we know the least about.

And a change has been made by the Department of Justice. Formerly, a person on court after-care supervision (a fancy term for parole) had to pass a urinalysis test every week or so, regardless of whether he was originally charged with a drug crime or not. If the individual failed the test he was sent back to prison on a violation. Now the policy is, upon failing the test, he is referred to a drug treatment program instead. An improvement, right? Wrong.

The problem is there are, at present, no crack-treatment programs, at least no effective ones. Current treatment modalities for crack have a 90 to 95 percent failure rate. Of the 5 percent who do remain drug-free for any length of time, I strongly suspect they would have done so without treatment. About one-tenth of 1 percent of crack abusers can quit on their own.

A superstar outfielder for the Los Angeles Dodgers learned the hard way how hard it is to stop abusing crack. Evidently he figured that since he had all winter off from his profession, he could indulge a bit. Came spring training and he was nowhere to be found. His club had to have someone drag him out of a crack house and into treatment. Now here's a man who gets paid millions for his services, and is in the public eye. Everyone is going to know about it if he screws up, but he still screws up. It has nothing to do with the man's character or moral fiber, anyone who plays around with crack will do the same thing this guy did. Virtually anyone. Anything for just one more blast.

The conclusion we have to come to is no one is strong enough to "just say no" once he begins using crack cocaine, and that's from the very first puff. Treatment modalities have to be developed with that thought in mind. Maybe one day researchers will come up with a "magic bullet" which will eliminate, or at least reduce, the irresistible craving for the drug, but until then the only treatment available is one which is pretty draconian, at least when compared to treatments for other additions.

I have to preface my treatment modality with the assurance that none of the following is meant to be punitive, it's just that nothing else works. A person cannot stop using crack by "free will." She has to be physically removed from access to the drug, which means an "inpatient" program. The standard inpatient programs (one month) are based on what works for alcoholics and opiate users, not crack abusers. It takes six months minimum under lock and key before the crack abuser has a ghost of a chance of even *beginning* to quit, when his dreams about getting high finally stop. Until that happens he is not in a proper state of mind to be amenable to treatment. After that, counseling can begin. Before this point I feel it is a waste of manpower to attempt counseling. The addict will mouth whatever he thinks the counselor wants to hear—and not mean a word of it. His mind will be attempting to develop a strategy to deal with the drug on his terms upon his release. He can't stop the thoughts from going through his head.

What should the addict be doing during this six months under lock and key? The smarter ones will attempt to keep themselves engaged in whatever activities are available, while the others will just sit there and pick their noses. Ideally recently closed military bases, which would probably fill up as fast as they were opened, will be utilized as camps for recovering addicts which will provide different physical activities.

After the six months is up, the person can be released with the understanding that she must attend drug counseling classes or self-help groups, along with *daily* urine testing. The *daily* testing is the whole key. Addicts' minds play games with them. They'll come up with all sorts of timetables about how they can do just one little hit and be "clean" before their next urine test. Daily testing is the only way to combat this, then they know they can't cheat. *They need and must have this kind of control in their lives.*

After a month or so of daily clean tests, they can be scheduled for a test every other day, then every third day, and so on. This has to be done over a period of at least another six months, with periodic testing thereafter for another five years. One dirty-urine result must mean they start the program over again from the beginning. This is not, I repeat *not,* a punitive measure, but is due to the nature of the drug. It takes only one hit to be back off to the races.

This is serious drug treatment which has a chance of working. At this point in time, anything short of this has very little chance of being effective.

There are methods to make the program a bit more palatable. For one, there are patches available (similar to nicotine patches) which will change color when someone uses drugs. This will eliminate the need (and cost) of extensive urine testing. Also roving counselors or lower-paid technicians can be utilized to visit individuals at their places of employment to check the patches. Why make a person lose hours from work to stand in a line with a bunch of other abusers to be checked? *This* is punitive, and counterproductive. Every dope dealer in town knows where the drug treatment centers are located and virtually all of them have a thriving dope business going on right outside the front door, or at least down the block. Addicts trying to kick shouldn't be exposed to this kind of stress. They just aren't that strong.

As to the costs of the program I've laid out, frankly, I haven't considered them. My only consideration has been what will possibly work. I'm not talking about a program with a lot of frills and gimmicks—they seem to add little, if anything, to successful treatment programs—but a basic program similar to the one I've outlined should be within our financial reach. If it is utilized by wealthy private industry it should be a matter only of this question: does society deem these individuals worth saving? I don't have the answer to that one.

Boot Camps for Brains

THE NEWEST WRINKLE in America's seemingly endless quest to discover effective means of deterring crime is prison boot camps. Young, first-time offenders are shipped off to these junior prisons—many of which are on the sites of recently closed military bases—to serve truncated sentences of six months or less in lieu of going to real prison.

Considering the helter-skelter, illogical reasoning behind most crime-prevention legislation concocted by politicians desperately grasping at any straw which even remotely sounds as if it has a chance of working, I can't help but wonder if the only logic behind this new scheme is the availability of the closed bases. A program designed to fit the excess space.

The boot-camp programs are supposed to foster discipline, which in turn is supposed to turn these young men away from lives of crime. Are the public officials who come up with these types of fuzzy programs merely misguided pointy-headed intellectuals or are they meanspirited conservatives who are once again instituting something which they know in advance is bound to fail? They take a premise which has an element of truth to it and use it to convince a gullible electorate they are really doing something on crime and thus deserve reelection.

While it stands to reason anyone would certainly benefit from keeping regular hours, eating a controlled diet, and getting plenty of vigorous exercise, to assume this will lead these young men to lives as productive citizens is complete nonsense. Without an education and a marketable job skill with which to earn a living, all boot camp will do is produce a stronger, sturdier, more disciplined breed of criminal who can outrun, jump, climb, and fight any cop in the city.

None of them will be able to earn a living from being well-conditioned upon their release unless they become Olympic runners. And no amount of discipline can prepare someone to starve in a land of plenty, or to willingly be reduced to asking the demeaning question, "Do you want a Coke with this burger and fries?" Grown men need grown men's work.

Judging from the level of excellence I see on the sports fields and weight piles at this institution, the young men who will be shipped to these boot camps will relish and thrive on the physical challenges. What makes overweight, middle-aged bureaucrats—who would do anything to avoid strenuous physical exertion—feel that this type of regimen will have a corrective or prohibitive effect on youthful offenders? They are enacting legislation which scares only them, not the young criminals.

These programs are designed to give a "second chance" to young men who have rarely had the first one. As the Attica convict said, "How the hell are we going to be *re*habilitated and we've never been habilitated in the first damn place?" Indeed. The programs will quickly come to be viewed by the young offenders as a means of outmaneuvering the criminal-justice system, at least on their first go 'round. Faced with the option of going to regular prison or a boot camp, the young felons will jump on the chance to go to camp like a dog on a bone. The judge, prosecutor, and probably the arresting officer will take this as a sign that the young person is truly sorry for his actions and sincerely plans to do better. They will go home feeling all warm and fuzzy about serving the ends of justice while saving a young person from a life of crime.

Initial indications from the boot camps already confirm that young, first-time offenders are just as likely to catch another case as men who don't get the benefit of society's supposed concern. What else did anyone expect? These young men come back out of the boot camps as unprepared for life in the real world as when they went in. But it doesn't have to be that way.

When no less respected an elected official than Senator Arlen Specter calls for rethinking the manner in which we attempt to rehabilitate first-time youthful offenders, the country should take notice. Senator Specter, who can't by any stretch of the imagination be considered soft on crime, is the first national politician from the right with the courage to speak the truth on the issue. Writing in the *New York Times* (January 4, 1994) Senator Specter rightly states that providing convicted felons with marketable job skills during their incarceration isn't coddling them; it's simply the best method of insuring they don't have to return to preying on society for their daily bread.

What our legislators need to institute are boot camps for brains. Over the last thirty years criminologists have increasingly abandoned prison-rehabilitation efforts as quite useless. Based on the percentage of convicts who return to prison, these experts have concluded that programs designed to reduce recidivism just don't work. I wonder how many of them have ever questioned their methods of administering such programs when casting about for a culprit on whom to pin the blame of failure? Or as usual, are the victims of ill-conceived programs blamed for their failure? They seem too easy and defenseless a target to miss.

The basic problem is that institutions which have incarceration as their primary mission can't do a very good, or even decent, job of educating. The mindset is entirely different, and all wrong. Prisons are places where anything other than basic warehousing is routinely denied to prisoners if possible. Staffs are practiced in the art of saying "no," and this doesn't change appreciably when it's education for which the convict is petitioning. The object is still to make it as difficult as possible, to erect as many barriers as they can between the convict and his goal. This is simply centuries-old prison culture at work. The current staffs didn't design the system, are not responsible for it, and certainly aren't able to change it. The convicts who obtain an education under these conditions are the tenacious ones. Those who aren't too thrilled by the education process—the ones most in need of it—aren't going to fare too well. And boot camps don't even pretend to offer education.

It's one thing to force young men to rise at the crack of dawn, double-time it to the chow hall, and then work and exercise vigorously all day; this can be forced. It's something else entirely to attempt to force them to learn something. You can lead a convict to the classroom, but you can't force him to drink of the enlightening water of education. Or can you?

I, for one, think you can if not exactly force at least coax youthful offenders into gaining an education while incarcerated, if that is the true goal of society and if society is willing, via its legislators, to make a reasoned and serious effort in this direction. It is my heartfelt opinion that no such effort has to date been made. Let's take a look at the situation.

The first hurdle which has to be cleared is the gaining of the young felon's attention, and the *only* method of doing this is via the courts. He has to know this release date is predicated on how soon and how well he acquires a marketable job skill. In most states sentences are already indeterminate. This means it is up to the parole board to determine whether a convict will serve the low or high end of say, a three-to-five-year sentence. The parole board's criteria is good behavior, maybe a point or two given for attending continuing education classes. When a marketable job skill is the bar convicts have to clear to obtain their release, believe me: you *will* have their attention. Simply because the school system failed to adequately prepare these young men to earn a living doesn't mean that we can't rectify this shortcoming now that the prison system has them. It is simply foolish not to.

Once, and if, society clears the first hurdle by deciding it truly is serious about not letting young men out of prison with no job skills (which virtually ensures they will one day hit someone over the head with a Louisville Slugger) then we can proceed to the next step.

All federal prisoners have to keep a job. My first job assignment, which I lobbied for, was assisting a staff teacher by tutoring convicts in the compulsory GED program. It's called a compulsory program because any convict coming into the institution who lacks a high-school diploma or equivalency is required to take the classes for 120 days. Not (I repeat) *not* necessarily graduate, just attend. They may sleep, or pick their noses, or more than likely pressure the prisoners who want to further their education to join them in dropping out of the process.

Within six months I was outta there. Two reasons. First, there is a financial nonincentive to being in the classroom as either tutor/convict or student/convict. My pay as a tutor was forty cents an hour and students were paid twenty-one cents an hour. The job I now have pays almost two dollars an hour. Admittedly not much, but a *huge* difference to someone locked up. It's the difference between maintaining some dignity in a prison environment and having to be a mendicant.

I'm somewhat lucky compared to many of the younger men here. I have a loving family who would provide me with the funds to purchase soap that doesn't make your skin break out, tooth powder which doesn't cause your gums to bleed, and an occasional treat from the commissary if I were to ask. (Okay, okay, I'll fess up, I get *lots* of treats from the commissary.) Many of the young men here are not so situated. But we're talking mere pennies—why not pay student/convicts wages comparable to those earned by the convicts who are sitting around the plumbing shop doing absolutely nothing? Remove one of the more obvious nonincentives to education. The young men are going to need a lot more than a high-school diploma if American society is serious about rehabilitating criminals.

While a few of the GED-class attendees are eager to learn, most are acutely embarrassed by having their educational shortcomings trumpeted all over the compound. They arrive in the classroom with a great big chip on their collective shoulders.

Now, before I continue, I want to make it completely clear that I am 110 percent behind equal-employment opportunities for women, but prison classrooms are one place where they don't belong. As I said, the convicts arrive with this chip on their shoulder, and even those who don't carry one around with them all too often do when confronted with a female teacher: they lust after her or attempt to disrespect her. Even those females who are strong enough to overcome the disrespect, and some can, still lose in the end because the convict simply shuts down and refuses to participate.

Staff teachers are rightly viewed as warders first and educators a distant second. It's only natural that tutor/convicts can more easily gain the confidence of student/convicts. One tutor/convict had a class he ran by himself. No staff member was present, and he was spectacularly success-ful. He had no discipline problems and he was able to cajole the most recalcitrant convicts into becoming amenable to the education process. I'm sure I could have duplicated his success had I been given the same situation.

It's a proven and accepted fact that ex-drug abusers oftentimes make the most effective drug-abuse counselors because they can better communi-cate with the individuals in need of counseling. They speak the same language, they are accepted because they've been there. The counselor and abuser have the commonality of a shared past and similar life experiences, and the same principles used in drug rehabilitation can be applied in prison rehabilitation.

At present, young inner-city blacks and browns are shipped to faraway locations and placed under the supervision of individuals with whom they have absolutely nothing in common, yet society expects this scenario to yield positive changes. As history and high recidivism rates have taught us, it can't. "Common sense," wrote Josh Billings, "is the knack of seeing things as they are and doing things as they ought to be done."

All of our rehabilitation efforts have been based on first securing an admission of guilt, whether actually stated or merely implied, from the felon as the first step toward change. Without this admission no serious effort is mounted by society to rehabilitate. The felon is deemed "not amenable to change." But society doesn't apologize to the felon for creating the conditions which cause him to be mired in poverty, which of course produces the crime. Rehabilitation is more than merely forcing someone to say "I'm sorry." Any serious rehabilitation efforts have to by-pass this finger-pointing toward whom or what is to blame for the felon's breaking the social contract. The disparate views and job skills of those in need of rehabilitation and those of the people who have historically attempted to provide change are never going to compatible. Using mature felons and ex-felons however, is a means of circumventing the question and the finger-pointing entirely.

The young felons should first go to boot camps for six to eight weeks just as in military basic training, then later they would go to another section of the camp for education. At this point, they would meet a "mentor" whom they can relate to. This is the critical point in the whole process. Unless the youngster can be reached at this time all subsequent efforts are for naught.

Bill Clinton has been calling on the black community to take a greater share of the responsibility for the crime and violence in its neighborhoods. What better way for blacks to positively impact on the problem than for the men who can potentially have the most influence on these young felons to be given the chance to do so? The benefits of such a program are doubled when we consider that this would provide jobs for recently and soon-to-be-released mature felons who otherwise would have difficulty obtaining employment. Are you listening, Mr. President?

Under the general supervision of prison officials, the mentor then would explain the facts of life to the young felon: true, we have a social system in this country which is riddled with institutionalized racism, but the only way to "beat" the system is to obtain an education and job skills. These young men need to ready themselves to start their own businesses, if indeed their anger prevents them from working or associating with whites. This is not about "being good"; it's about being successful. How did Malcom X rise out of prison to be a leader of his people? Through education. Continued fighting of the system through lawbreaking will only result in the lawbreakers' spending the majority of their lives incarcerated. The black race sorely needs for our youths to get their act together if we are ever to overcome the racism which played a large part in the incarceration in the first place.

Now, not all of the young felons are going to respond positively to this message immediately. Some will undoubtedly have to be recycled back through the boot-camp phase, but still they should be made to realize that they are being afforded a serious opportunity to overcome their shortcomings in order to gain much-needed skills. They need to know that the program is designed to spend as long as necessary insuring they get the message, their whole sentence if necessary.

Even the best designed and carried-out program will not be able to reach all of the young men who are currently lost. We have to be ready to accept this fact, and society has a right to protect itself against their committing other acts of violence. Once these young men are provided with job skills, potential employers should be given tax credits as an incentive to hire them and thus give them the chance they have so far been denied. Those who still continue to break the social contract by committing acts of violence should then be taken to long-term prisons and locked away. Forever.

THE DUEL

DUELING AS A METHOD of settling disputes fell into disfavor over a century ago. However, I think due to the present climate in America we should take another look at the archaic practice.

Dueling came into existence in A.D. 590 in the Burgundy region of France under King Gundobad. He reasoned that since his subjects were willing to risk their souls by lying under oath during court proceedings they may as well risk their bodies as well; thus "Trial by Combat," "The Judgement of God," and "Trial by Ordeal," as dueling variously was known, came into being. The murder and mugging rates in Burgundy declined immediately upon its inception.

The practice quickly spread to other kingdoms until the Catholic Church, concerned about jurisprudence of the sword challenging that of the rule of the altar, attempted to outlaw it. The church passed an edict against dueling in 1041 and threatened to excommunicate any sovereign who allowed the practice to continue in his realm. The church, however, was largely ignored. It continued to try to ban the practice over the years and at the councils of Valence, Limoges, and Trent it further reinforced its stance.

It was not until Henry II of England (1133–1189), in an attempt to gain favor for his newly instituted "trial by jury," did a ban on dueling have any real effect. But still the practice persisted in England until Parliament outlawed it in 1819. Dueling, however, had undergone many transformations by then.

During the Middle Ages, the practice of hiring "champions" to fight in one's stead had become popular in certain countries. The practice of allowing the challenged individual to select the weapons originated in England around the time gunpowder become popular. In the mid-eighteenth century, Andrea Alciati, an Italian theoretician and fencing master,

master, codified dueling for the first time, setting down strict standards and rules which gentlemen were expected to observe. Dueling was imported to America where it eventually mutated into the Wild West phenomenon of gunfighting.

I give this brief history in support of what some will no doubt consider a barbaric suggestion. However, in spite of the sullied reputation the practice garnered it was a worthwhile means of keeping the peace, as I shall endeavor to demonstrate. When a man could challenge another man to account for his actions on the "Field of Honor" the need to do so occurred far less often. Men respected each other more. They had good incentive to do so.

The demise of dueling had little to with its lack of utility. The introduction of "champions" into the practice played a large part in changing attitudes towards dueling, for then the rich man could disrespect someone with impunity and simply hire the best fighter around to take care of the matter for him. It is also interesting to note that the rise of the robber barons coincided with dueling's decline. When men felt they could get away with anything they generally did.

An excellent example of how respect would be restored if dueling were revived can be seen in prison. Here men from different backgrounds, who would probably get into a knock-down, drag-out fight if they rudely bumped into each other or stepped on each other's toes on the street, are quick to apologize. The rule is give the other guy, black or white, big or small, some respect. And the reason for the rule is simple: if you fail to he can make you pay and pay immediately. There is no place to hide in prison, at least not for long. If you wrong someone, even a little shrimp of a guy, he can come up behind you with a shank and set matters straight.

Dueling had much the same effect. People respected each other or paid the price. No hiding behind high-price lawyers; no using the courts for cover after the fact, just "meet me in the street, motherfucker."

Will this result in people calling each other out on a daily basis? Not likely. What it will result in is people not giving other people a reason to call them out. R-E-S-P-E-C-T.

The number of people currently taking violent revenge against what they perceive to be a system which ignores the individual and his grievances is growing. Mass shootings are becoming a daily occurrence. The enraged employee or client, often unable to focus solely on the object of his wrath, takes it out wholesale on everyone nearby when he finally does go off.

I submit that if we still practiced dueling this would not be occurring. The wronged individual could approach the person who disrespected him, slap his face, and tell him to choose his weapon. Just knowing you could get the satisfaction of challenging someone in that manner would have the effect of giving adequate vent to violent emotions.

An island offshore where dueling was allowed could serve to circumvent present prohibitions. Instead of seething inside, a person could tell the obnoxious and overbearing boss or cheating insurance-company claims agent, "Meet me on Duel Island, you lily-livered coward." It would be better than shooting up the whole neighborhood, at any rate.

PART
V

POLITICS, MEDIA, AND THE SOCIAL ORDER

CLINTON TO THE RESCUE?

COME QUICKLY, 1996, for I have little choice but to cling to the belief Bill Clinton, after (and if) he has won reelection, will begin to govern with conscience rather than with the dictates of political expediency.

He has stated that the worst period in his life was when he was forced to sit on the political sidelines after being voted out of the Arkansas governor's mansion in the early eighties. He made a vow then he would never again allow his conscience, espousing what he knows to be right, true, and just, get in the way of his winning an election, and he hasn't. While this may sound downright Machiavellian, he seriously took to heart the lesson that a politician who caters to the public whim and wins still has a better chance of influencing policy than one who speaks his mind and is voted out of office.

I'm sorely hoping Clinton is simply telling the public what it wants to hear in terms of the recent crime legislation to win reelection. Then it would follow that during his second term he would mature into his own man and administer the bitter medicine the country must swallow if we are to ever cure our ills in the areas of crime, drug abuse, and violence. His first step in that direction would have to be a five-year trial-decriminalization of drugs. This continued treating of a medical, social, and economic problem with legal means will eventually bankrupt the country while continuing to needlessly destroy lives in the process. If a person has cancer and is treated with heart medication he will undoubtedly soon succumb.

Steven B. Duke, a Yale law professor, and Albert C. Gross, an attorney, cite in their book *America's Longest War* that the savings from such a move, in terms of dollars, could top 200 billion dollars a year. The savings in terms of human suffering and lives (due to sharply reduced prices of drugs, the main reason for the killings) are virtually incalculable.

This one act would achieve more, in terms of insuring America remains strong and economically viable, than any other single action could hope to accomplish. But it is an action which has to be "sold" to the American public. And it can be.

The idea that Americans will not go along with decriminalization is pure hogwash. American public opinion is so malleable it can easily be manipulated by the media, which can, if it chooses to, sell coals in Newcastle, ice in Alaska, and sunshine in Hawaii. All the media has to do is start showing white youths being arrested and sentenced to draconian prison terms for small amounts of drugs (as currently happens to blacks) and watch how fast the American public will go along with decriminalization of drugs.

For years the American public has bought into the idea that we can solve our drug problems by building more prisons and sentencing more people to occupy them. If they'll believe this illogical policy will work then they'll believe *anything*. And make no mistake about the media's willingness to forge this change in public opinion; it only awaits the word from on high, which so far hasn't been forthcoming.

Only Kurt L. Schmoke, the politically savvy mayor of Baltimore, has so far had the courage to state publicly what many politicians will state only in private: our drug laws and policies are insane. They should be administered by the Surgeon General, not the Attorney General.

Mayor Schmoke, who had a bright political future and was being considered for statewide office, knowingly sacrificed those opportunities by taking the stand he has. He knows right-wing politicians would crucify him on this issue statewide, all the while knowing his position is the only sane one. By boldly speaking the truth on this issue, Mayor Schmoke has put public policy ahead of personal political gain. He is risking all to pave the way for Bill Clinton, playing John the Baptist to Clinton's Jesus if you will, to follow him after Clinton has safely won his second term as president.

I hope that the cavalry, in the form of other politicians and opinion-makers, will soon arrive to assist Mayor Schmoke in holding the fort until Clinton can saddle up, which won't be until after the 1996 elections. I'm just praying Clinton will have the courage to then do so.

CRIME AND COMMUNISM

IN THE WORLD of national politics, crime has become the new Communism. Politicians, at a loss for an issue on which they can rise on the floors of the House and Senate and express righteous indignation, have seized on crime, much like Joe McCarthy seized on Communism as the "red menace" forty years ago.

Not that crime isn't an issue which needs immediate addressing, it definitely is. But in a responsible manner, since a reasoned approach is more likely to produce the desired results—the reduction of crime—than plain old demagoguery. No other issue on the national agenda is subject to as much manipulation, muddled thinking, and illogical oratory as crime. And while all of this pontificating serves our politicians well in terms of getting them reelected, it does nothing to actually reduce crime. But, since candidates discovered the vote-producing potential in scaring the bejeebers out of the electorate, crime has become a national football. So much so that if all serious crime were to magically disappear overnight our elected officials would have to increase the penalties for lesser crimes, such as jaywalking or dropping a gum wrapper, to continue to have a political vehicle to ride back to their sinecures in Washington.

Crime is too perfect an issue for them to ever let go of, even if it continues to decline as, according to FBI statistics, it did last year. Those convicted of crimes lose their right to vote, and other than FAMM (Families Against Mandatory Minimums), a Washington-based group headed by Julie Stewart, have no lobbyists. All of this would be laughable, except to victims of crime, if it wasn't for one fact: the more politicians use the issue as a reelection vehicle, the less the chances workable solutions, which actually reduce crime, will be implemented.

If, as our politicians constantly tell us, enacting stiffer sentences and building more prisons would reduce crime we, by now, would be a crime-free nation. The hard, cold fact is, the methods our nation has utilized in the last twenty or so years (while maybe satisfying to the national sense of retribution) have failed to reduce crime. More of the same measures will also fail to work.

Crime, being the emotional issue it is, lends itself perfectly to all sorts of specious solutions. In virtually every other area of national concern, Congress consults experts in the given field and, after thorough questioning, adopts the experts' opinions and codifies them into law. Only with crime is expert opinion solicited and then totally ignored.

Everyone in Congress (and every other level of government) is an instant expert on crime the minute he gets elected. Which, of course, begs the question, with so many experts around why aren't their solutions working? Why is crime still a growing concern? Part of the reason is (and I know how outlandish this sounds) many politicians don't really care if the solutions work or not—where else could they get such a ready-made issue? Their main concern is not so much solutions, but issues to run on. As such, they are addicted to crime.

Two tragic incidents of last year, one in Petaluma, California, the other in St. Louis, both involving the kidnapping and murdering of young girls, resulted, as they certainly should have, in a public outcry to protect our children. The sad part is tougher laws on the books won't deter the next sick person who can't resist his impulses. Treatment is needed *before* he commit his heinous deeds, not after. This is called crime prevention, building more prisons to house criminals after the fact isn't.

The FBI issued a profile of the killer in the St. Louis case (the California killer has been captured) and as usual in these types of crimes, he is thought to be an adult white male. Over the years these profiles have been so highly developed their accuracy is nothing short of amazing. In this area, the experts are listened to with rapt attention. Yet the end result of the public outrage, as likely as not, will be more young, inner-city blacks being arrested for car theft or selling crack. How this will protect our nation's children from being harmed I don't know. But then, neither does Congress.

Vote for Me and I'll Set You Free

BLACK MAYORS, it seems, are cropping up all over the landscape. Even in cities with majority white populations, such as Denver and Seattle, blacks have been able to wrest control of city halls from white politicians.

At first glance, this trend would seem to denote a lessening of racism on the part of whites in major population centers, and the judgment of black politicians by the content of their character rather than the color of their skin. Since this is what blacks have marched, fought, and died for, it would follow that these elections should be reason for rejoicing in the black community. But not everyone is joining the chorus.

One has to take a look below the surface of these supposed "victories" for black candidates and see what Faustian bargains were struck by these black men, who were extremely hungry for elective office, with white voters. What campaign promises did they make (or imply) to convince the white electorate they were indeed the right men, at the right time, in the right place?

Could it have been these black candidates promised to keep the "natives" quiet and under control in the black ghettos so whites could get a good night's sleep? Well, considering that crime is, thanks to the media (which has managed to assure the public crime is running rampant) much on the public consciousness, it would seem the white citizen would be willing to vote for a black candidate if she felt it would help make her safer. But then, a white candidate can demagogue the crime issue as well, or better, than a black candidate. No, I don't think it's the crime issue.

Let's see, what other issue arouses emotions as much as crime among whites? What other single issue has virtually every city in America wrestled with for the last twenty years, often sparking riots and other social upheavals? You guessed it, bussing.

Yes, bussing. The one issue where a black political candidate can out-demagogue a white candidate hands down. If a white candidate dares to suggest an end to this controversial practice, he is derided as a racist. However, when a *black* candidate suggests basically the same thing, as all of the new black mayors have done, he is embraced as a savior, at least by his white constituency. What these black candidates learned to do was to make their position on bussing acceptable to the black community. They already were a leg up with any propositions they put forth since most blacks are so eager to have one of their own in a highly visible elective position, they are fairly easy for black politicians to manipulate.

Since whites remained unalterably opposed to bussing over the years, many blacks have become weary with the issue. They began to wonder if the fox was worth the chase. It is relatively easy for a black politician to tell them, playing on their racial pride, that they don't need to have their children sit alongside a white child to get a decent education. Wouldn't it be better, asks the black candidate, to concentrate our efforts on improving the schools in our communities rather than keep fighting for something which probably isn't worth very much anyway?

From my perspective, having black children sit next to whites has always been secondary to the issue of where the school funds were going. Only a extremely naive person would believe that white-dominated school boards haven't historically allocated funds for everything from building maintenance to new computers in an unfair and disproportionate manner. Mixing the races is the only sure method I know of to counteract this.

Let's face it: black and white children will, as long as America remains as racist as it is, self-segregate at the onset of puberty no matter what anyone does. Even those black and white children who start kindergarten together will, once the sexual myths begin to flourish, become like oil and water. Just look at majority white college campuses. If they at least go through the primary grades together, then the demystifying process will have taken place. The awe and fear they would hold for each other by virtue of never having any real contact will have been dissipated. And this is a giant and necessary step if the races are to coexist in America.

What the election of these black mayors should wake us up to is the fact that, like their white counterparts, these men are so hungry for political gain they will make any deal, sell out any issue, forfeit any birthright, simply to get elected. They are not black saints. What good does it do for blacks to have one of their own in political office if the elected official has had to make a deal with the white establishment to ignore the needs of his race to get elected?

PITY OUR POOR POLITICIANS?

ROBERT RENO, in an article written for *Newsday*, lamented our parsimoniousness in regard to congressional salaries. His reasoning followed the predictable path which leads others, in industry, commerce, and finance, to incomes of half a million dollars a year and more, while our national legislators earn a supposedly paltry $133,600, and are just as competent as their private sector counterparts. Naturally, there are those who would debate Mr. Reno on the question of parity of competency.

He also feared that if we continue to scrutinize every wart, blemish, and pimple on these public officials' private lives, in the not-too-distant future we will be "governed exclusively by millionaire hobbyists, crooks, and eccentric losers." Again Mr. Reno could engender spirited debate since many feel this is the type of Congress we are already saddled with.

However, I concur on this latter point; we certainly don't have a right to hold our politicians up to a light so glaring no one could pass muster without being singed. But he is wrong to suggest that this overly rigorous examination is being carried out at the public behest, it's not. Instead, he should be addressing his comments to his fellow journalists. It is they who tear into candidates' pasts like packs of wolves, gleefully exposing any tidbit of irrelevant information as if the "revelation" is going to gain them a Pulitzer Prize. They force-feed us this drivel and exculpate themselves by loudly proclaiming "the public *demands* to know!" when actually it is them demanding to tell us, whether we want to know or not.

The newly awakened public demand for politicians to be more responsible legislators has been twisted and reapplied to their personal lives until we all seem to be nothing but a bunch of Peeping Toms. The media do this simply to sell newspapers or attract viewers to pseudo-television news programs.

Their strange bedfellows in this public undressing of candidates are the piranhnic media consultants and campaign coordinators hired by the candidates, people who vie to outdo one another in digging up dirt on the opposition. Since the candidates eagerly spend millions of dollars and will make any Faustian bargain to win a job which pays only a bit more than $100,000, their "handlers" (read: manipulators) rightly reason no depth is too low to sink to in the quest for a political victory. The desire to run other people's lives, it seems, indeed runs deep.

Huey Long once stated he could win reelection as long as he "didn't get caught in bed with a dead woman or a live boy." He was probably right, since he did what a politician is supposed to do: make his constitutents' lives appreciably better. Despite his rough-and-tumble reputation, he was also a statesman, something we haven't seen in this country (with the possible exception of Senator George Mitchell) since Hubert Humphrey retired. Statesmen aren't afraid to take an unpopular stand in the cause of what is right.

Mr. Reno also wrote that we "have a collective fit" over free congressional parking at the National Airport. This demonstrates his lack of insight into the public mind. It isn't the fact that the parking is free which rankles the public so much; it's the fact that the prime spaces are the closest ones to the terminal. The symbolism of the lot—which bespeaks a privileged ruling class somehow too good to trek through a parking lot like us common folk—far outweighs the fact of the restricted parking area. If our congressional members were indeed sensitive to our feelings, they would change the situation. They would use parking valets like all other people in a hurry who don't care to take long hikes. There is something patently un-American about "special privileges."

Rather than make the job more attractive as Mr. Reno seemed to be suggesting I would prefer we make it less so; maybe we should be making *them* pay *us* for the privilege of running up trillions of dollars of debt. As it currently stands there are already far too many people whoring after a limited number of high political offices. They will sell any lie, promise any moon, do virtually anything to gain election; and after they are elected they only get worse.

Many of our present national problems can be directly traced to our politicians making and passing laws they know infringe on the rights of minority citizens. These measures, which won't and can't work, are enacted for one reason, and one reason only: to ingratiate the politicians with the majority electorate. They'll violate their consciences with impunity, trample any rights of minorities, and twist the Bill of Rights every which way but loose to gain the votes needed for reelection. If opinion polls indicated that the majority of voters were in favor of bringing back burning at the stake politicians would quickly enact the legislation, complete with reasonable-sounding rhetoric to justify their spineless behavior. They have lost sight of the fact that leaders are by definition supposed to lead. If that means sometimes taking an unpopular, vote-costing stand because it is the right thing to do, then so be it.

But how many of our national leaders have enough courage to even blow their own noses without looking to see how the voters will react, let alone stand up like statesmen when majority public opinion is wrong (as it often is) and say, "No! This is not right!"?

TWO DIFFERENT PROGRAMS

TWO RECENT NEWS ARTICLES illustrate the disparate approaches being used to address the problems of the underclass. One works; the other, while having some minor success, doesn't.

The first is an ambitious program which has been in limited use in Chicago since 1976. When a federal judge ordered an end to high-rise projects construction, citing the fact that they are mere breeding grounds for crime, a group called the Leadership Council for Metropolitan Open Communities was funded by the Department of Housing and Urban Development (HUD) to disperse the residents of the projects throughout Chicago and its suburbs.

The program has produced some major success stories. Free from the everyday specter of crime and violence, able at last to attend decent schools, most of the children of these relocated families have gone on to achievements they never could have dreamed of while living in the ghetto.

Henry Cisneros, the dynamic but overly scrutinized minority member secretary of HUD, has plans to vastly expand the successful program. He has stated in no uncertain terms that the only thing to do with the projects is to tear them down. However, once white politicians—who never before worried about the program since it was so limited—realize the extent of the changes Mr. Cisneros envisions, they are going to move vigorously to block his efforts. They will fear that these blacks, who are currently crammed into these ghettos, will begin to disperse throughout their all-white enclaves. The fear of integration is indeed still strong in America.

Political expediency would seem to dictate that as many of these minorities be relocated to working and middle-class black neighborhoods as possible. Not only will the relocated families feel more comfortable, but white fears—and it is hoped white opposition to the program—will also be reduced.

173

The goal of the program is not to punish whites for their past discrimination by moving in black families, even though that is what many whites will no doubt feel. Its sole purpose is to improve the lot of underclass blacks. Certainly some of the black families will have to be relocated to white neighborhoods; if too many of them are placed in black communities other ghettos will be created, thus defeating the aim of the program.

Personally, I would prefer to see all of the underclass dispersed into middle-class black neighborhoods, but due to racism, past and present, there simply aren't enough of these neighborhoods to absorb them all. Whites should view these blacks moving into their communities not as punishment for their racism, but merely as by-products of it. One can only pray that when the inevitable fight over this program occurs, that Mr. Cisneros has the political clout to come out on the winning end of it.

The other news story concerns the closing (supposedly only temporarily) of a boot camp in Connecticut. While a few of the young men who went through the program had some degree of success (obtaining their GEDs), the facility was plagued with gang activity and marijuana use.

The boot camp was staffed with ex-military men who could utilize their training to impart some discipline to the young men who had run afoul of the law. On paper I guess it looked like a pretty good program to those who conceived of it. However, the flaws should have been obvious from the outset.

For three decades, from the fifties through the seventies, errant youths were inducted into the military as an alternative to going to prison, and the strategy usually worked. Many youngsters' lives were straightened out by the experience. The reason this worked and the boot camps can't is that being inducted into the military causes a inner-city youth to become absorbed by an already-established culture. His peers become positive role models and influences on his life.

In the boot-camp situation his peers all were from the ghetto and had the same values, or lack of them. They brought their culture with them. The fact that some leaders were present in the camps simply wasn't enough to prevent the youths from inculcating their old habits and ways into the new environs. Leadership provides the overall atmosphere, but the actual changes in behavior are accomplished through peer pressure, something the leadership can't provide.

The boot-camp concept has a much better chance of being successful if an "exponential" type of program is used. A smaller number of the best candidates should be put through the program, sort of on a "buddy plan."

The best of these should be retained as group leaders for the candidates who follow. The ratio of staff (or young men who have already successfully completed the program) to inductees has to be relatively high, otherwise behavior changes won't occur. However, once enough young men have gone through the program it can grow exponentially.

The trained ex-military men—who were in all probability virtually all white in the Connecticut boot camp—have to be used to being in supervisory positions (if enough blacks can't be found) and their presence gradually lessened as more blacks and other minorities take over the running of the programs. It's just a plain fact of American culture that young ghetto blacks and Latinos are going to be distrustful of whites, and, at least in their minds, with good reason. Winning their trust is half of the battle, and someone of their own race and culture can do this much more quickly and effectively.

SHOOTING OURSELVES
IN THE FOOT

MY FATHER GAVE ME my first .22 rifle when I was seven. On fall weekends he'd take my brother and me down to a deserted slag heap about five miles from our inner-city home where he taught us to shoot. By age ten I had my first .410 shotgun with which he taught me to hunt rabbit and pheasant.

Since we lived upstairs over the tavern he owned in a rough neighborhood on the east side of Cleveland, I grew up accustomed to seeing a handgun around at all times. He had a matched set of .45 army Colts, one of which he kept in a nightstand drawer beside his bed and the other in a drawer beside the cash register in the tavern. Since he'd let me handle both guns at an early age, even letting me fire one of them on New Year's Eve, I wasn't very curious about them. He always stressed firearm safety and it simply never occurred to me to even touch, let alone handle, either of his guns without his permission. He didn't keep them under lock and key since if trouble broke out he'd need to be able to get to them in a hurry. It was that kind of neighborhood. He also had confidence in his teaching ability: he knew we would never touch his guns. Times, and we, were different forty years ago.

If I were to have a male child I doubt seriously if I would even allow him to play with toy guns, let alone the real thing. While some would call me a wimp for my attitude and point out the fact that my father taught me the proper way to handle firearms, I would still be opposed to it. Like I said, times were different then.

A gun was viewed as a peace-keeper or sporting tool by my father, nothing more. And I still hold to the views I was taught. But today angry young people without the faintest inkling of the concepts of responsibility, conscience, or remorse, buy, sell, and trade guns as youth of my day did bubblegum cards. The isolation and estrangement of individuals caused by our fast-paced world are causing more and more of them to plunge off the edge into madness. And with the ready availability of powerful weapons like Uzis, unknown in past generations, they can, and do, wreak havoc on society. There may, in fact, be no more people going nuts today than before, they are just better armed.

In the short term, even with strong antigun legislation, we are not going to experience a decrease in handgun violence. There are just too many weapons in circulation. But we have to start somewhere to counteract the Wild West mentality which permeates our culture. That will take time, but I would start with my own child.

However, when a problem gets out of hand in our society our attempts to correct it always do some harm to a number of unintended victims. Let me illustrate.

A fellow convict named Will is sixty years old. As a callow youth of nineteen he stole a car. Since it was his first offense he was given probation and never got anything more serious than a speeding ticket since. In fact, it was a speeding ticket which began his current woes.

It seems he was stopped for speeding while on his way home from a hunting trip. His shotgun was laying across the backseat of his car. Three hours later he was arrested by the ATF for being an ex-felon in possession of a firearm. The police called out of curiosity (and the desire to get a pat on the back) to see if he'd ever been arrested. He's doing five years.

Next is Jim. He also had a youthful indiscretion: along with two other college buddies, he broke into a liquor store and took three kegs of beer so their after-hours beer bash wouldn't have to come to an abrupt end. They left the money for the beer on the counter. And even though they paid the repair costs to the door when captured, they were still convicted of breaking and entering, which they should have been. Twenty years later Jim called the police to the neighborhood deli he and his wife had recently purchased to quell a disturbance outside. The police, after doing their duty, came inside to talk with the new owner they had yet to meet. They saw a handgun in plain sight near the cash register (it was a tough section of the city) and even though it was registered to Jim's wife he is now also doing five years: another ex-felon with a firearm.

The last guy, also in prison with me, is a real desperado: he sold an informant two dime bags of marijuana and when the cops couldn't find the mountain of drugs the informant told them he was sitting on, they looked in a dresser drawer and found a gun. Even though it was an old gun and was in pieces in a cigar box, had been for as long as he could remember, no matter. He still got seven years for possession of a firearm during a drug transaction.

I know you think I'm making these stories up. I thought the same thing until I began helping these guys with their cases and read the details for myself. As draconian and unfair as they sound they, unfortunately, are all too real. Is this what the new laws were designed to do? Make bitter men of two former solid citizens and a harmless doper?

In times past two of the three men would have been warned, at worst, to file an exemption with the ATF to be able to possess a gun. In the third case, the guy would have been charged with selling the two dime bags, a misdemeanor. The guns would have been ignored. But federal prosecutors are now eager to make their bottom lines look better at the end of the month, so they allow these cheap-shot cases. After all, they *do* involve guns. They're known as "dead-bang" convictions since they are so easy to win.

When, years down the road, we hear the gun laws aren't doing what they were supposed to do, think about these men and you won't have to wonder why they aren't doing the job.

WHO ASKED YOU? NOBODY!

ONE OF THE MAJOR REASONS most of the social programs of the last thirty years which deal with the problems of the underclass have, by and large, failed, is the seeming inability of those who formulate these policies to take into account the views of those whom the programs are designed to assist.

There exists a very real bias against any consultation with the members of the group who could, if given the opportunity, add overlooked insights into the viability of the various plans which are supposed to solve the problems of crime, teenage births, substance abuse, and poverty.

A number of reasons exist for this omission. Chief among them is the resentment the average citizen feels for having to shell out tax dollars for these purposes. He feels that asking the people who are the recipients of these funds what they believe needs to be done only adds insult to injury. There is also the feeling among social scientists that "we know what's best for you." This feeling is based on the premise that since the people of the underclass are in the condition they are in, they obviously don't know what to do to get out of it. This leads to attempts to apply solutions which would probably work well for middle-class people. The problem is, these people are not middle class.

Additionally, there is the "communications problem." The two classes of individuals speak entirely different languages. To be sure, both languages are English, but social mores and cultural differences make meaningful communications difficult. And most professionals in a given field are disdainful of those who cannot speak the jargon of that field. It matters little that the results these "experts" have produced in the last three decades are less than spectacular; if you can't speak in their arcane tongue and couch your meanings in esoteric academic phraseology, the chances of your thoughts being given any serious consideration are indeed slim.

While all of this exclusion may be very satisfying in a perverse way, to those who hold the purse strings to the social programs, it isn't a very effective method of solving the problems our society is faced with in this arena. The idea that the victims of these poorly formulated programs can be blamed for their ultimate failure (thus letting the "experts" off the hook) when the solutions don't work goes a long way toward keeping members of groups most affected out of the American Dream.

Common sense dictates that everyone who could offer input into the best way to solve these social problems, thereby better utilizing the dollars spent in attempting to raise the standard of living for the underclass, should be seriously listened to. The costs associated with continually maintaining an ongoing underclass are staggering. Also, more and more citizens, while they fully understand there is a problem out there, are becoming less inclined to shoulder the burden for the programs. Times, it seems, are tough all over.

Because of a lack of organizational skills, most of the groups formed by people of the underclass have had very little impact. Without the means to hire public relations firms to put a positive spin on their public statements, most Americans view the efforts of these groups as being an attempt to increase the amount they receive while on the dole. Rarely is it understood that these people are attempting to offer input which, if factored into the equation, would help provide long-term solutions.

Part of what reinforces the cycle of poverty is the feeling that one has no control over any aspect of his or her life. Most people, when dictated a solution in which they have little or no input in formulating, will have little incentive to see the program work. This is human nature.

Isn't it about time our leaders sent someone around to ask the criminal what it would have taken to have kept him from becoming one? Why not ask the welfare mother what kind of help she needs to get off of welfare? Why not talk to the substance abuser about what kind of program he thinks would prevent another generation of young people from throwing their lives away?

If the programs currently in use or being proposed were working, or had a glimmer of a chance to work, proceeding as we have for years would seem the best course, but they're not. To proceed with more programs without including the members of the underclass in their design is not only wrong-headed, it's also guaranteed to squander resources better used to find tenable solutions.

SPARE THE ROD, SPOIL THE CHILD

IT HAD TO HAPPEN. Everyone should have seen it coming. It was too "hot" an issue (read: one out of which political hay can be made) for some politician not to jump on.

I'm talking about the Orange County, California, supervisor who has proposed, in the wake of the Michael Fay caning incident in Singapore, that corporal punishment be instituted into our legal system for youthful offenders. The supervisor, however, is proposing an additional twist: public floggings, or "paddlings," as he so euphemistically calls them.

The potential embarrassment, according to this armchair behavioral expert, would deter youths from going astray. "Spare the rod, spoil the child," and all that platitudinous nonsense. Too little too late, is my response.

I can't say that I myself didn't use corporal punishment when my children were small. The most recent incident was a few years back though. My granddaughter—who was about three at the time—had accompanied me on the short walk to the local supermarket. While I was placing the items in the cart I had to tell her twice to come away from the bins which were filled with loosely wrapped penny candy, conveniently placed at a child's eye level and reach for the purposes of enticement, I suppose. As we walked home, with her trailing behind me, I looked back just as a piece of candy was falling out of her pocket. I looked farther back and a trail of candy was strung along the ground. Some thief.

I questioned her, attempting to discover the depth of her awareness of right and wrong about taking something which didn't belong to her. Her attempts at prevarication were weak at best: she was a precocious child, and of course she knew the difference between buying and stealing.

I informed her mother of the incident and told my granddaughter Catie we would have to return to the supermarket where she would make a clean breast of things to the manager, a woman she knew well. I then swatted her rear with a few halfhearted whacks, using my voice to express my displeasure more than my hand. One criminal in the family was enough, thank you.

I think the swatting, along with the trip back to the supermarket, had the desired effect. Catie doesn't take things which don't belong to her anymore. But, as I said, she was three at the time and her personality was still forming. To attempt to correct the failed products of our (certainly someone's!) neglect with corporal punishment after they've reached young adulthood is an exercise in futility. How much the supervisor, or anyone else, expects this method to work and how much of it is simply an attempt at self-satisfying retribution is hard to determine. But since we are near the end of our collective ropes in terms of coming to grips with crime, violence, and general disrespect for the law, I am willing to go along with a try at corporal punishment, with one caveat: we use it on adults also, and publicly.

Certainly the Orange County supervisor had in mind paddling only those youth who spray graffiti on walls and other such public nuisances. But what about the crimes committed behind closed doors, undercover? Aren't they just as harmful to society?

The bank official who redlines neighborhoods, thus depriving blacks of equal-housing opportunities; the policeman who gets up on the witness stand and "testifies" simply because he has a "gut" feeling, but little evidence, that the individual on trial is guilty as charged; or the employer or manager who blatantly commits sexual or racial discrimination on a daily basis? Shouldn't these crimes also be covered, or is the good supervisor suggesting only people of certain ages (or maybe races) be subjected to this ridiculous, humiliating, and worthless form of punishment?

I imagine it matters little to the supervisor that the Singapore policemen supposedly used tactics on Mr. Fay's two alleged accomplices which were reminiscent of the methods used by Göering and Himmler to extract a confession. After breaking one's ribs and puncturing the other's eardrum, they still wanted to cane them!

What asinine schemes like the one the supervisor proposes actually do (other than enhance his chances of reelection) is prevent us from dealing rationally and effectively with crime and punishment. It plays to our emotions in a disgusting manner. But the problems of our society run much deeper, I'm afraid, than mere public humiliation can readily rectify. I truly wish it were as simple as paddling people.

AH, SINGAPORE

AH, SINGAPORE, that garden spot of the East. The purposeful caning of an eighteen year old American youth by authorities there has brought the differences between our two societies into sharp relief.

The fact that the young man was, as of this writing, scheduled to be beaten (caning is only a nice euphemism) by a martial-arts expert to the extent it will probably send him into shock and leave permanent scars, has polarized American opinion on the issue. Our government has protested to officials there that the punishment is far too severe for a nonviolent prank (spraying paint on cars) but since Singapore depends little on U.S. largess, the protests have, to this point, fallen on deaf ears. The situation however has escalated to a war of words with the retired president of the country chastening our diplomats for questioning their human rights record when crime is rampant in our streets. I think he meant something to the effect of "stones and glass houses."

Many in this country applaud the sentence as right, just, and necessary. They only wish our courts would emulate Singaporean justice. They cite the amazingly low crime rates as proof that authoritarian methods of crime prevention do indeed work. And at first glance, they seem to be right. In Singapore there were but fifty-eight murders in all of 1993, versus 1,063 for Los Angeles during the same period. Only three cases of robbery with a weapon out of 1,008 versus 38,167 for its American counterpart. Graffiti is unknown, as well as street gangs. Women can walk the streets alone unmolested at any hour of the day or night. Sounds like heaven, right?

Even minor infractions, such as jaywalking, can get the offender a $500 fine, the same as the fine for chewing gum in certain towns. Any society which knows how to curtail this activity can't be all bad. Those caught littering face public humiliation and ridicule—something we definitely should look into here.

Serious crime is punished swiftly and harshly. Armed robbers and drug dealers face a death sentence from which there is little chance of appeal. The courts there have no rules against self-incrimination, and they have no jury-trial system. The judge's word is final; punishment is swift.

Many Americans would be willing to give up some of the liberties and safeguards we enjoy in return for some peace and safety, and who can blame them? But everything in life is a trade-off; you give up one thing to gain another. However, one thing all the articles concerning the differences in our two cultures fail to mention is that there is no graft or public corruption of officials there. They don't have one set of rules for the citizens and another for the leaders of the country as we do here. Everyone is expected to abide by the same rules. How our public officials would react to giving up their perks, lobbyists' "favors," and outright payoffs is hard to determine. They might go into a form of shock themselves. In the private sector, insider trading would get the perpetrator maybe twenty years and a very sore ass. Price-fixing and rigged bidding would also be subjected to stern penalties. The "old boy" network would have to be completely dismantled.

The reason there is no crime in Singapore is not due to the harsh penalties. The penalties are so severe simply because there is no reason for anyone to commit a crime. What prevents crime in their society is full employment under a fair and just system. What everyone fails to understand is there is no poverty in Singapore!

They have a basically homogeneous culture. Discrimination, if it occurred, would be punished as harshly as other antisocial behavior. In a society which treats everyone equally and fairly, you can more easily justify harsh penalties for those who break the social contract. In a country with no slums and underclass it is relatively easy to have low crime rates; criminals aren't bred like so much cattle. They simply don't tolerate conditions which breed crime and violence.

Now, are Americans willing to give up their cherished prejudices in order to have a peaceful and orderly society? I know that's going a little bit far, expecting maybe a little too much, but hey, like I said, everything is a trade-off. I'm willing to give up some of my rights, agree to punish criminals just as swiftly as they do in Singapore just as soon as America is willing to give up its racism, the root cause of crime. Something tells me this is a deal which America just isn't willing to make.

SIDESTREAM CAFFEINE

THE TOBACCO COMPANIES are finally beginning to catch the hell they deserve for causing 400,000 smoking-related deaths a year and then lying through their teeth about the culpability of their products. Even though I'm entering my fourth decade of addiction to cigarettes, I relish the manner in which Congressman Waxman of California and a few other members of Congress are taking on one of the strongest lobbies in America, and coming away with some important victories. They know that keeping the public eye focused on the problem is the surest way to bring people to their senses about this disgusting habit.

Here in federal prison cigarettes are sixty cents a pack, due to the fact that there are no federal taxes to be paid on them. I wish the tax was raised so high that the price of a pack, both here and in the street, would go to more than five dollars. Maybe then weak-willed people like myself would finally find the courage to quit this pernicious practice.

Interestingly, when smoking first started to gain popularity in Europe a few countries enacted strict laws against the use of tobacco. In one or two places a person could be put to death if caught lighting up. Evidently those ancients knew something about the damage smoking does to a society that we are yet to learn.

The tobacco companies are using every dirty trick in their overstuffed book to put a good spin on their current problems. The latest move is to equate the proposed limits which are being considered for the advertising and sale of tobacco products with a loss of liberty. One ad states that maybe caffeine will be next, as if anyone was ever harmed by "sidestream caffeine."

The bad old days when special-interests lobbyists for harmful products held ironclad sway over our legislators as their industries polluted, poisoned, and killed us are coming to a none-too-soon close. The once powerful and feared gun lobby is being forced into a hasty retreat as their handpicked candidates lose elections and recall efforts against those politicians who oppose them fail.

The liquor industry will be next. No one in their right mind would suggest we return to Prohibition; it didn't work then and it won't work now. But alcohol is a deadly killer which has to be deglamorized and portrayed for what it is. Both the liquor and tobacco industries have targeted minorities to increase sales of their deadly products. As the products' damage to society became more widely known, and their actions subject to stronger challenge, they consciously selected segments of the population they felt would engender the least amount of criticism and offer the least resistance to their spread of sickness, despair, and death. They increased their advertising in these markets with predictable results.

As the tobacco interests continue to suffer setbacks they are beginning to mount extensive advertising campaigns in Third World and developing countries. It seems the thought of using their vast resources to enter other, less harmful, markets has never once crossed their money-grubbing little minds.

In the Watts ghetto of Los Angeles there were, before the Rodney King riots, more liquor stores than exist in the whole state of Pennsylvania. Maxine Waters, the congresswoman for the district, defied the Rebuild L.A. Committee and powerful Asian interests by refusing to allow most of the liquor stores to be rebuilt. The statistics are grim indeed: 30,000 people die each year in alcohol-related auto accidents; 100,000 die annually from other alcohol-related injuries and illnesses; 75 percent of all murders in the country involve alcohol; and alcohol plays a major factor in spousal and child abuse.

When the total picture of alcohol-caused devastation is taken into consideration, the fact that we allow this industry to pander to our youth with their diabolically clever opinion-shaping advertisements is virtually criminal. Their advertisements, which portray alcohol as being a necessary ingredient to having the good life, never give our young people a chance to make reasoned, informed choices about drinking. Getting drunk is still considered big fun in too many high schools and on too many college campuses. This has to change.

Especially in the black community. Already saddled with every social problem imaginable, we can ill-afford to offer up another generation of our children to be crucified on the mantle of corporate profits. If they're going to be targeted, then we have to give them added defenses in the way of more education.

One proposal, to increase the taxes on alcohol, has so far met with industry resistance even though it has been proven that when the price of alcohol goes up drinking goes down. The additional tax revenues could be put to good use combatting the problems these industries create in our society.

The real question is, how much free reign are we to going to give industries which sell and glorify the use of toxic products, even in a free society?

DOCTORS OF DEATH

GEORGE BERNARD SHAW, in his 1906 preface to his play *Major Barbara*, wrote, "The state is constantly forcing the consciences of men by violence and cruelty. Not content with exacting money from us for the maintenance of its soldiers and policemen, its galoers and executioners, it forces us to take an active personal part in its proceedings on pain of becoming ourselves the victims of its violence."

When the hangman or the ax wielder did his grisly deed there could be no uncertainty as to who was responsible for the dispatching; only his identity remained shrouded in a black hood. With the advent of the firing squad, every man who aimed his rifle at the target pinned over the victim's heart could exculpate his conscience by virtue of the fact that one of the guns was randomly loaded with a blank.

I've heard that when electrocution came into use, some of the contraptions the condemned were strapped into were wired to three separate switches; only one of them actually supplied the electricity which often sent smoke shooting from the victim's head. Again, the three men flipping the switches could absolve themselves of guilt. Gas chambers were often designed for the pellets to be dropped by a timer, as if the device alone was responsible for the dastardly act.

Now we are back to square one: only one person can shoulder the responsibility for inserting the needle into an arm of the victim of a lethal injection. I wonder if that individual wears a hood? If he does, once it comes off some would be amazed, shocked, and then angered to discover a doctor underneath, a member of the profession which is supposedly dedicated to saving lives, not taking them. Formerly, doctors were usually in attendance at state-sanctioned killings to check the pulse of the condemned after the fact and to certify that the deed had been carried out. But now the doctor is himself the doer of the deed. This is appalling.

That a person who has taken the Hippocratic Oath allows the state to use her to put a sanitized and painless face on barbarism is causing consternation in some quarters of the medical profession. The American College of Physicians and Physicians for Human Rights, have joined with the National Coalition to Abolish the Death Penalty and Human Rights Watch to protest this perversion of the healing profession. A study entitled *Breach of Trust*, which calls for physicians not to participate in the practice, has recently been made public.

However, there will always be some quack somewhere with a medical degree who will provide his services to the state as society is pushed back toward the primordial ooze from whence we came. Since no one wants to be known to be associated with the act, the states pay the doctors in cash. If the death penalty were accepted nationally, the number of greedy physicians (who would just love to make a little extra pin money which doesn't have to be reported) lined up at the prisons prepared, nay clamoring, to carry out the supreme sentences probably would be shamefully long. As the amount of work for these potential ghouls increases, so should the pressure on them to resist this practice, continue from citizens and from their colleagues. They should be ostracized, if not outright stripped of their licenses to practice medicine.

If we are going to continue to engage in a practice which we normally associate with the countries of the world we like to look down our noses at as "barbaric," then we should kill proudly and openly. Make the judges and juries who mete out these sentences carry them out themselves, publicly. Think of the ratings televised executions would gather! If we're going to do evil, then goddamn it, let's do evil in prime time for all the world to see. Enough of this Janus-like hiding of the darker side of the American psyche. As Shaw wrote, "If a man cannot look evil in the face without illusion, he will never know what it really is, or combat it effectively."

LIFE AS A BALLGAME

CURRENTLY A GREAT HUE and cry can be heard throughout the land for other states and also the feds to follow the lead of the state of Washington and enact tough, new "three strikes and you're out" legislation. The law mandates life sentences, without the possibility of parole, for a third felony. In some states the legislation is a bit more reasonable and covers only a third violent felony. As anyone faintly familiar with the criminal-justice system can tell you, prosecutors are going to have a field day magically turning property crimes into violent felonies simply to threaten someone with life and to get guilty pleas. And guess what the skin colors of most of these individuals will be?

In some cases, three strikes are two strikes too many, but when such strong measures are passed, equally strong safeguards should be instituted to insure the laws are applied fairly and equably. As it now stands, blacks suffer the death penalty at a rate twenty-seven times that of a white convicted of the same crime. What do these new laws portend for blacks? Recently one young black man who was about to be executed was so mentally deficient and unaware of what was transpiring he wanted to save his pecan pie from his last meal for later.

I hope no one is naive enough to think such tougher laws alone will actually reduce crime, because they won't. During the eighteenth century pickpockets in England were publicly hanged. During the hangings, which attracted huge crowds, other pickpockets were working the audience. So much for deterrence via legislation. Removal of violent felons who prey on society, however, is something any sane country has a right and duty to perform. They must be isolated until they are old enough to no longer pose a threat to anyone. What we have to guard against is the wrongheaded public taste for revenge. While revenge is not a laudatory emotion, it is all too often the impetus for changes in our laws. The feeling of retribution which flows outward from pontificating politicians to the general public may be temporarily gratifying, but does little in the long run to reduce crime. Maybe people feel that since deterrence doesn't work they might as well settle for revenge.

The problem is, when new, tougher laws are enacted new rules of engagement also go into effect on the mean streets. Criminals faced with losing their freedom forever if caught and convicted of their third purse snatching might now start carrying guns to shoot it out with police or, as will more likely occur, shoot the hapless victim who either resists or dares to raise a cry. It's called "holding court in the street."

Another factor comes into play which the general public doesn't realize: those who are charged with administering the laws immediately find ways around them when it suits their purposes. It's called "prosecutorial discretion" and it means the prosecutor has a wide degree of latitude in selecting which category he places a crime. Say, a kindly, old child-molesting priest gets knocked for the third time. Is this his third violent felony? Maybe so, maybe not.

Let me construct a scenario for you which is not too farfetched: a twenty-one year old guy gets into a barroom fight and breaks the bouncer's nose. He's convicted of felonious assault. Strike one. Ten years later he's married, but things are not going too well in the marriage. He gets his bowling ball out of the closet and heads for the door, only to find his path blocked by his wife who accuses him of going to meet his girlfriend. He pushes her aside to leave and she falls and bruises her leg. She calls the cops and he's convicted again for felonious assault. Strike two. Now this guy had better be damn careful for the rest of his life or he could spend it in prison. If my created character happens to be black. . . .

Will the newly proposed laws remove some violent felons from society who have forfeited their right to freedom? Certainly. Will it allow others who should be removed to sometimes go free? Without a doubt. Will it incarcerate for life some who don't deserve it? You can bet your life on it.

THROW AWAY THE KEY!

THE "THROW AWAY THE KEY"LOBBY is at it again. First some nitwit connected with Lucasville Prison in southern Ohio proposed to remove all of the weights from the prisoners' exercise yard, and now a county supervisor in a Wisconsin community is on to the same bright idea. He wants to remove the weights from the county jail. While he cites the fact that he feels buffed-up prisoners pose a danger to the guards as the reason for his proposed actions, he also stupidly let the cat out the bag when he let it be known that his real intentions were punitive: he stated that phones and televisions would be the next items on his list to go. One would have to wonder what danger these two prisoner "privileges" pose to the guards? Are the convicts going to become stronger by flipping the channels of the television or lifting the receiver of the telephone? And even if all the convicts became veritable Atlases, they would still be no match for the riot shotguns the guards would break out in case of trouble.

Of course his concern for the welfare of the guards is only a smoke-screen. Additional punishment is what he is really after. Convicts have it too good he feels. That, and the probable fact that the guys who make these proposals are little wimps who have trouble lifting their wives' petticoats. If they can cane prisoners in Singapore we can at least make it a little tougher on them here, is their rationale.

Don't these clucks realize penologists are among the most competent professionals in the world? They should be. They have a captive group of people who have little recourse but to go along with whatever ideas they devise, and so far none of the professionals has come out in support of these asinine measures. Their reasoning for remaining silent is quite simple.

These measures are largely unenforceable. The professionals might be able to get away with them for a while, but eventually the men are going to buck. The proverbial crap is going to hit the fan. The solution to this conflict would be to increase force against the convicts, which would only cause the convicts to buck even more. An ever-increasing, life-threatening struggle of wills would result. Rather than make institutions safer for guards, their measures would actually make them more dangerous. But then, these armchair hardnoses won't be the ones doing the enforcing.

No guard can safely manage twenty-five convicts without their cooperation. And when you have literally hundreds of men massed in a chow hall, the potential for a riot is frightening—to both convicts and staff. The "privileges" are the instruments the guards use to control the convicts. The weight pile works off the inmates' tension and the television and telephones serve to act as baby-sitters. The threat of curtailing these "privileges" acts as a carrot; remove these and you remove all incentive for inmates to cooperate.

When penologists first wanted to air-condition housing units there was a hue and cry of "convict coddling," but that just wasn't the case. The penologists found that convicts who are kept in housing units where the temperature is below seventy degrees are far less prone to argue and fight. They are too busy keeping warm. Every summer in unair-conditioned, overcrowded jails, all hell breaks loose when the thermometer cracks ninety degrees. And the guards are expected to wade into the melee and restore order.

The guards who work at these institutions know full well what works and what doesn't. The problem is they can't speak up and tell the administrative boneheads what they think of their ideas for fear of jeopardizing their jobs by sounding weak or on the side of the convicts. These guys are already doing a job few in society would care to do, they don't need for someone sitting in a plush office somewhere to make it any tougher for them.

Those who make these proposals should first educate themselves in penology before making any suggestions. Then they should first test their draconian proposals on themselves, or stick to their knitting.

The Plea, Please

FURTHER PROOF OF THE NEED to address the inconsistencies and unfairness of the criminal justice system can be found in the method by which the majority of criminal cases are adjudicated.

The plea bargain, which is used in every court in the land, is used to keep court caseloads at manageable levels. Since a district attorney's office in a busy metropolitan area may process 10,000 criminal cases a year through courts which can handle only 1,000 jury trials a year at best, some bargaining has to go on somewhere.

This is also the stage where selective enforcement has been elevated to a fine art. If, say, an overzealous cop has stopped a white kid for buying dope from a black kid in a bad neighborhood and instead of giving him a scolding and sending him packing, which is the usual practice, the cop arrests him, this is the point where he'll probably walk on it. It is up to the prosecutor to decide what charge, if any, will be brought. The white kid, at this point, usually gets to go home while the black kid who sold him the dope gets to plea bargain, since selling dope is worse than buying it. However, if the situation is reversed, and say it's the white kid who is selling the dope, then he is usually still released since the logic will also be reversed and now the black kid who bought the dope is the bigger threat to society.

The deal is struck by the lawyer for the black kid, who is now known as the "defendant." The defendant will stand in front of a judge and the judge will solemnly ask him if anyone has promised him anything in return for his guilty plea. The defendant will then answer no, which everyone in the courtroom knows is a lie. The prosecutor, via the defendant's lawyer, has promised to either drop other charges, reduce some charges, recommend a lighter sentence to the judge, or stand mute at sentencing, or any combination of the foregoing for the guilty plea. This is the bargain. Yet no one raises an eyebrow when the defendant stands there and tells the bald-faced lie. It's all part of business as usual.

And the deal is sweetened to insure the defendant will take it, or made more punitive if he doesn't. It works like this: say the crime the defendant is charged with carries a sentence of ten years. If the defendant "pleads out" to the charge, he will receive something like two years, maybe less than that. But, if he chooses to exercise his right to a trial by jury—which is every citizen's right—and he is convicted, he will then receive the full ten-year sentence, plus something will no doubt be inserted into his file to let the parole board know he wouldn't play the game so they too can stretch him out.

What, you may ask, is wrong with this? Justice is served and the defendant gets a deal. This is what is known as a "win-win" situation, right? Not quite. This system makes a mockery of justice. It impresses on young defendants the fact that courts and due process are simply a charade. How will they ever learn to respect the law when the law doesn't respect itself? A quibbling point you may feel, nitpicking. Not so.

To correct this situation only requires that plea bargains be officially acknowledged by the courts. The judge, instead of asking if something has been promised to the defendant, would simply ask if the defendant completely understands and is satisfied with the deal. No big thing at all. Then why doesn't the court simply do it that way?

Your guess, dear reader, is as good as mine. The only conclusion I can come to is the courts operate with a "we've got you now you sonofabitch, and we'll do it any damn way we please" attitude. After all, who can make the courts change the way they operate? Which is just my point. If the courts can flaunt the Constitution and their own rules at will on small matters, what's to stop them from doing the exact same thing on larger issues?

The road to full partnership in the American Dream for blacks, by necessity, goes directly through the courts. If we can't receive justice there, where can we? What looks like a simple thing—almost an oversight—however, is telling. Most of those facing plea bargains are blacks or minorities. If the courts don't think enough of our rights to correct such a simple matter, how can we expect them to make larger adjustments when necessary to serve the ends of justice? Due process is due process, and blacks have to learn to demand it at every step or it will be overlooked, and then soon denied.

THE COURT OF LAST APPEAL

SINCE THE SIXTIES, according to a March, 1994, story distributed by the *New York Times* News Service, the number of lawsuits filed by prison inmates has grown from just a few hundred a year to more than 33,000 in 1993. And I could swear I've read every one of them.

Because I spend most evenings in the typing room of the prison law library working on one writing project or another, and, since I'm prematurely gray—ipso facto—I know something about the law. Or at least that's what many of the young convicts coming into the system with too long sentences wish to believe. And I do know a little about the law. Damn little. However, since the prisoners seeking my assistance know even less, and many don't possess decent reading skills, "in the land of the blind a one-eyed man is king."

At first I attempted to dissuade the young dudes by claiming total ignorance of the law, but that didn't work. They just got mad at me and claimed I didn't want to help a brother. After I made the mistake of writing two simple letters to the courts for a couple of prisoners and got favorable responses to some minor matters (which the court clerks had probably overlooked), I was considered the black F. Lee Bailey of the compound. There was just no way some of these guys were taking no for an answer.

Luckily, there is a real lawyer who works in the reading library who gives me advice on some of the trickier points of law and makes sure I'm headed in the right general direction. I tried to get the young men to deal directly with him but since he is white, and the guy who put them in here is usually also white, well, you get the point.

No one mentions the many times I wrote the court or filed a suit and got blown out of the water; they remember only my few victories. Hope springs eternal in the hearts of men.

Yesterday I wrote a letter to the "region," the office of the regional director of the Bureau of Prisons. A newly arrived convict wanted to get transferred to a prison closer to home. I didn't even bother trying to inform him his chances of a transfer before serving six months here is zip. I simply cranked out my now standard spiel about family hardships, wishing to maintain family ties, etc. But the convict is happy, because he's doing something and feels he's fighting. I put the book of stamps he paid me with in my locker, which is bulging with all sorts of goodies I get paid with for being the patron saint of lost convict causes. But if I had told him the truth I would have been the villain. Why? Because I'm here. He can see me. He can't see the guy who is going to shoot him down at the region.

The point is the vast majority of prisoner suits *are* frivolous. Some are worse than that. The *Times* article cited Thomas J. McAvoy, the chief judge of the U.S. District Court in Albany, New York, by quoting, "I mean, 70 percent of these [people] don't even state a complaint of which relief can be granted." I've sure typed my share of those kinds of turkeys.

I do two types of legal work. In some cases I look up the applicable case law, frame the appeal in logical legalese, and then type it up. In other cases, I simply type up what the convict has written, mistakes, busted verbs, and all. At first I would clean up the prisoner's English, correct spelling, check punctuation, the whole nine yards. However, after more than one prisoner accused me of tampering with their "expert" work and threatened to make me wear my ass for a hat, I began typing verbatim.

Judge McAvoy and others want to limit the number and types of appeals convicts can file. Recently the Supreme Court has had to grapple with the rising flood of death-row appeals. I can sympathize with their frustration over what they consider a wasteful use of the court personnel, but to limit appeals would have a chilling effect on the whole redress process. Who would decide which issues are worth being heard?

The article also stated that many of the improvements in prison conditions (the right to worship mostly by Muslims, the right to access to law books, better diet) which make institutions safer for everyone by reducing tensions have been the direct result of convict-inspired lawsuits. To disallow lawsuits based on some as-yet-to-be-determined criteria for judging merit would cause more problems than it would solve.

Prisoner lawsuits make up about 15 percent of the federal civil-suit docket. Who is to say the other 85 percent all have merit? The whole point is that two or more people disagree. That's what judges are for.

Americans love to litigate. We have more lawyers per capita than any other country in the world. Our courts are overflowing with cases. It is understandable officials want to do away with some of the mountains of paperwork, and it's equally understandable that convict suits are the logical target. But which class of suits will next be deemed not worthy of being heard? Discrimination suits? Sexual-harassment cases? One of the hallmarks of our form of government is that *everyone* can seek redress in a court of law. I can sue you if I don't like the color of your eyes. While this sounds ridiculous it's one of the nuisances we have to put up with to protect the rest of our rights.

Whether people care to admit it or not, prisoners have rights, too. If prisoners' suits are curtailed, prison officials will have a field day taking away prisoners' rights. This of course won't disturb some people; they feel prisoners have too many rights as it is. But what they fail to realize is the courts are the last resort for some men. It is the only hope they have. Take away a man's only and last hope and you'll have a dangerous man on your hands. The courts act as a safety valve. Some men follow prison rules only because they feel they are eventually going to get some relief in court some day. The prison murder rate will shoot through the roof. This, again, won't bother some people. At least until the guards start dying. In reality, the staffs of institutions run prisons only because the convicts let them. Convicts choose not to rebel because they have the courts for redress of the grievances. The courts should be careful or they'll make an already precarious situation impossible.

SOUTH AFRICA!

THE POSITIVE WIND OF CHANGE blowing so refreshingly across South Africa heralds a new day of hope for people of color throughout the world. The demise of apartheid comes just in time for a new, fairer political system to be erected in that strife-torn land, in time to meet the dawn of the twenty-first century.

However, as much as these changes gladden the hearts of all blacks (as well as all other right-thinking people throughout the world), many black- and brown-skinned people are still living under the heel of oppression in their adopted countries. To hope that the whites of these countries would willingly follow the wise lead of the white South Africans and attempt to construct truly pluralistic societies is probably hoping for too much. Many of the world leaders who attended the jubilant swearing-in ceremonies of Nelson Mandela returned to their own countries and continued policies of unofficial apartheid.

Even Fidel Castro, whom the American journalists were dismayed to see embraced so warmly by the officials of the African National Congress (thus showing their monumental ignorance of world affairs since they should know Cuba was virtually the only country in the world to support the South African struggle by offering armed assistance), can be accused of allowing racism to exist within his revolution. His "workers' paradise" never really overcame the tendency of the previous Battista regime to exclude darker-skinned Cubans from full participation in that supposedly egalitarian society. So much for leftist politics solving the problems of the black race.

Racism is allopatric. In the larger cities of England the increasingly strident cry of "England for the English" can be heard. Similar right-wing movements can be found in Germany, and, to a lesser extent, in France.

The fallout from past centuries of colonialism is catching up to these so-called democracies. "So-called" because to most minorities Western democracy is a bitter joke. For years these once-great powers exploited the darker countries of the world, and now the bill is coming due in the form of an influx of "unwanted foreigners." Except in many cases these "foreigners" are second-, third-, and fourth-generation citizens of these countries.

During their imperialist phases England, France, and Germany invaded and settled stolen lands, attempting to make them over into their own images. They made these distant (nearby in the case of France and Algeria) points of the globe part of their empires; appropriated vast sums of wealth in the forms of natural resources, cheap labor, and expanded markets; and now want nothing more to do with them.

When these low-birthrate nations needed cheap labor to bolster their workforces (and thereby maintain their standards of living) they welcomed the indigenous people of these lands with open arms to perform the tasks none of their citizens wanted to do. Now that recession has set in, they wish to make these newer citizens the scapegoats for all of their national ills and frustrations. They wish to make them disappear.

No doubt many a white American now rues the slave-trading days in our past when millions of blacks were brought to these shores through the dreaded Middle Passage. If they could have foreseen the social problems they were creating for the country down the road they certainly would have found another method of empire-building rather than the use of slave labor. Their shortsightedness then can only be matched by their shortsightedness now as they fail to forthrightly address current unrest created by mistakes centuries in the making. We, your darker-skinned brothers, cannot simply be "wished" away.

South Africa was faced with a crisis. The cry for freedom was so powerful and the scourge of apartheid was causing so much turmoil within the country that no one, neither white nor black, was able to enjoy the peaceful progress all men seek. Something had to be done.

F. W. deKlerk wisely joined with Nelson Mandela to bring about an end to the most iniquitous system of government the world has ever known. He did it for two reasons: the whites would get no peace if he didn't, and, there is enough wealth in that land for everyone. There was simply no economic justification for the oppression of one portion of the the citizenry to enhance the prosperity of the other. All citizens of a country can, and must, be provided with the opportunity to prosper if peace is to reign supreme. America would do well to take a lesson from the recent events in South Africa. The small-minded nonsense propagated by white racists in this country has set our national racial policies back for far too long. It has to now be relegated to the historical trash heap of outmoded thinking. How long will we continue to allow our country to remain in strife simply to satisfy the racial prejudices of latter-day Kluxers and workaday bigots?

One day a president will have to gather the courage to do the right thing: tell the country that its treatment of minorities is no longer acceptable. Never mind the fact that our police officials attempt to categorize the violence occurring in our inner cities as simply underclass crime, as if this fact justifies our being locked out of prosperity. Let the real truth be known: these are the rumblings of people struggling, in the only manner known and left to them, to be free.

I, like many others, wish South Africa godspeed along the road to peaceful, full equality. I pray black Americans' time is not too far behind.

PART
VI

WORDS AND ADMONITIONS FOR BLACK AMERICA

Economic Pressure

THE INTENTION OF THE SLAVE TRADERS who brought my ancestors to this country wasn't to hate, or even ridicule, them. They neither despised nor vilified my race. Their motives were purely economic in origin. Racism developed after the Civil War when whites saw they could no longer profit from us as much as they formerly had. They felt they had to develop a vehicle to keep us oppressed and deprived, and the system they devised is still, after all these years, proving effective. Our problem still boils down to one thing: money, or more accurately, the lack of it. Once we solve the economic riddle this country poses to us we'll improve our lot substantially. Not that whites may like or respect us any more than they do now, but at least we won't be so affected by their feelings. Now we are either viewed as a problem or completely ignored.

The following is a letter I wrote to a marketing company which uses television advertising extensively:

Dear Sir or Madam:

I've noticed the commercial your company runs for a telephone headset features a dozen individuals using your product in various circumstances, yet none of them are African American or other minorities.

Since I can't imagine your company not wishing for minorities to purchase the product also, I was wondering why your ad doesn't reflect the diversity of America. The new generation of black consumers, I assure you, notices such slights and oversights.

They will no longer support companies or products which deny their existence by omitting them from commercials. Personally, I would not buy that product or any other from your company until such time as the oversight is corrected.

Sincerely,

I received exactly the reply I expected: none at all. After all, if they looked at the return address, which is mandatory on all of my correspondence, they could tell I'm a prison inmate and therefore probably a nut to boot. However, about three months later I saw another advertisement from the same company for a child's toy and—lo and behold!—right there in the middle of the group of children was a black face! Fleeting though it was, nevertheless it was there. Was this in response to my letter? Probably not. No doubt they were planning on bringing their commercials into the twentieth century all along without my prodding. I don't need the credit for encouraging them to do so; just the end result that it was done is satisfaction enough for me. I even crafted my letter in a manner which let them off the hook for overt and purposeful racism by using "oversight."

But on second thought, I am going to take the credit for it just because it makes me feel so good and will encourage me to continue to write others when I'm confronted with racism in any form or shape. Never mind what the receivers of my letters think about me; they have to be told in no uncertain terms we are not going to sit placidly by and be ignored on camera when someone is soliciting our business. And you, and you, and you, too, should be writing letters right along with me; fair, pointed, and exact ones which let these people know how we all feel.

As a child I was always embarrassed whenever, on a shopping trip downtown with my hat-and-gloved mother, she would quickly and firmly let the mostly Eastern European sales clerks know she wasn't about to put up with any nonsense from them. This was in the early fifties. More than once my mother would, in her best voice, say "My ancestors have been in this country for over 400 years and if you can't show proper respect while waiting on me, I'll see if I can arrange to have you shipped right back to the old country on the next avaliable boat!" That usually worked quite well.

A recent survey showed black women pay the most for new cars, followed by white women, and then black men. Of course, the white male pays the least. Since blacks historically earn less than whites anyway, we certainly can't continue to allow ourselves to be taken advantage of in this manner. We need to form strong, black, economic consumer organizations to make the impact of our dollars felt. Of course we should, until racism abates in this country, purchase only from other blacks whenever possible, or at least boycott companies that do not represent, hire, and respect our race.

Caveat emptor has always existed in the marketplace; it is just a fact of black life in America that it exists more for us than anyone else. It's about time we began to actively defend ourselves economically en masse.

CRIME CONFERENCE— NO CRIMINALS ALLOWED

JESSE JACKSON'S RAINBOW COALITION held a national conference on crime in Washington this past January. *USA Today* did a large feature on it (while the other papers, which love to trumpet rising crime rates to increase circulation, for some reason didn't deem this effort by blacks to come up with solutions to crime newsworthy enough to cover) and quoted black criminologists, politicians, entertainers, and athletes about the problems of youth violence and black-on-black crime.

The statements ran the spectrum from the incisive (Wilhemina Delco, a Texas state representative, who stated "Our pat middle-class answers don't work in this [poor black] community") to the meanspirited (Ken Hamblin, a black Denver radio talk show host billed sometimes as the "black Rush Limbaugh," who felt black youths should be shipped to desert prisons to work in the sun so they will, out of fear of the conditions, quit committing crimes. I don't suppose Mr. Hamblin would care to take the job guarding these young men under such conditions.). Conspicuous by their absence from the conference on crime were some real experts on crime, and what it will take to stop it: criminals or former criminals.

A side panel accompanying the article featured profiles of two cities, Washington, D.C. and Gary, Indiana, did however, solicit comments from residents of the neighborhoods where a good deal of the crime occurs. Most prominent in their replies was the consensus that the youths responsible for the majority of the crime pay little attention to the black media stars who hope to influence them.

This should come as no surprise to anyone since most middle-class blacks have worked assiduously for years to distance themselves from their brethren of the underclass. Now that the problems (which to some

207

degree have grown in direct proportion to the amount of neglect displayed by blacks who should have been reaching back to help the less fortunate members of their race long ago) have gotten out of hand, these ghettoized blacks, rightly or wrongly, don't trust those middle-class blacks. They feel these blacks are being trotted out by the white power structure to "quiet the natives."

This arm's-length approach to the problems of the underclass (as well as to the members of the underclass themselves) by middle-class blacks just won't work. As distasteful as middle-class blacks might find the proposition, the only way they are going to be able to affect the problem is to go where the problem occurs: the ghetto. One thing's for sure: as much as they might dislike this, they would view the prospect of poor blacks visiting them in their safe enclaves with even less enthusiasm.

One of the standard jokes of the poor black community is that when members of the underclass must interact with the white power structure, be it something as simple as getting a phone bill straightened out, they would prefer the person they deal with to be white, since they feel their chances of being "dogged" are far greater with a black functionary.

Ken Thompson, a black hospital maintenance worker who was interviewed for the *USA Today* story, spent twenty years in prison. He felt many ex-convicts could do a better job of counseling inner-city youths than degreed professionals of either race. He decried the fact that many ex-felons have gone on to get college degrees but still aren't utilized enough to help deter the next generation of black youths from getting involved in crime. This lack of utilization is often due to some blacks being unwilling to include reformed criminals in their efforts, no matter how much they could contribute.

From a personal perspective, even though when I'm dressed in a suit and tie I can pass for a lawyer or doctor (being a former perpetrator of fraud, on occasion I had to), I know which spoon and fork to use, don't pick my nose in public, and haven't busted a verb in years, I still would have been unwelcome at the conference on crime once my background was known. There would have been the excellent chance I would have been treated as badly as the most menacing, doo-rag-wearing gang member. However, *both* I and the gang member should have been given an opportunity to be heard.

Whether our lack of welcome would have been due to jealousy that my opinions might carry greater weight with youths than theirs, or if the professional civil-rights workers, who have made a career out of supposedly monitoring and influencing the thoughts and actions of all blacks, would have feared competition for the access to the ears of those in decision-making positions, I don't know. What I do know is that anyone who can make a contribution towards solving the problems of the under-class should be encouraged to participate in the quest for solutions. Now that middle-class blacks are getting involved they shouldn't make the same mistake as whites: making decisions *for* underclass blacks instead of *with* them.

THE BLACK CONSERVATIVE

A STRANGE BREED of animal, the black conservative. His decided tilt towards the right end of the political spectrum amazes, and often angers, many other blacks who hold the more liberal views traditionally associated with the disenfranchised of our country. But these right-leaning anomalies have always been around, and, in truth, have basically the same goals and aspirations for the race as other blacks, though they manifest them in sometimes strange and different ways. What liberal and conservative blacks disagree on are the root causes of our problems and the best method to solve them.

Most blacks tend to become more conservative with age. However, many black conservatives are relatively young and most often come from families where right-wing or highly religious views are a long-held tradition. In fact, my father was a Republican.

Black conservatives tend to view the problems of the black underclass as the result of inherent, or at least strongly established, character flaws rather than the conditions of racism. They feel that problems could be overcome if "those people" would just somehow repair their defective moral compasses. They echo and give succor to the white conservative view that poor black individuals should be able to "will" themselves out of their plight to a better life.

The conservatives wonder how dare these denizens of the nation's ghettos demand equal treatment and rights when they are doing so much wrong? If they would simply stop the boozing, drugging, partying, and general slothfulness they too would be able to make something out of their lives. So goes conservative orthodoxy of all races.

Of course, the black liberal takes another view of the problem entirely: stop the racism, oppression, and blaming the victims of these social crimes for their condition and the problems of the underclass would soon disappear.

Both groups may agree on certain facets of the issue though. There can be little debate about the damage teen pregnancies are doing to our race. However, rarely does liberal and conservative agreement go much beyond that point. Conservatives see it as a matter of volition: these youths should simply abstain from sex until they are adults and safely married. End of problem. But, like the white, conservative, religious fundamentalist, conservative blacks aren't above using scare tactics to achieve their goals.

They're from the "God will get you" school of morality and gleefully predict agonizing deaths due to AIDS and other plagues too horrible to mention, which He has sent as punishment for all who defy Him. They attempt to convince youths that the sex act itself—even between two uninfected individuals—is capable of producing AIDS because God don't play that shit.

Black liberals, on the other hand, place their faith in accurate sex education, coupled with an attempt to convince these at-risk youths to avoid behavior which could harm their futures. The problem of course is, too many of the youth don't have futures to protect. Since these methods are meeting with mixed success, black conservatives believe it is time we use the methods of moral stormtroopers.

At the heart of the differences between black liberals and conservatives is the issue of white culpability, i.e., what role white racism has played in creating and perpetuating the horrible conditions too many blacks live under. The black liberal accuses the black conservative of allowing himself to be used by whites to justify their racist, reactionary views. They view the black conservative as little more than modern-day "house niggers."

Some validity to this view is seen by the operations of a black conservative political group known as Project 21. It is white-financed and the chairman is a twenty-three-year-old white from Long Island. It seems the white conservatives don't trust their black "friends" to be smart enough to run their own organization. Its stated goals are to spread the word that organizations like the NAACP don't represent the mainstream of blacks in this country, who, according to them, are happy as clams with the way things are going.

As I said at the beginning, these conservative blacks want the same things for the black race as more liberal blacks. And I meant that when I wrote it. Now that I review this essay, I'm not so sure I can allow them the luxury of that much benefit of a doubt. I also said they have a strange way of getting there. They damn sure do.

WHETHER INTEGRATION

ONE OF THE PERSONAL PROBLEMS racism creates is paranoia. When I read or view something I feel smacks of bigotry, I have to always do a quick reality check: am I judging this fairly? Am I overreacting? Could the sender of the message mean something other than what I'm perceiving? It's damn tiring.

And I have other things I'd rather spend my time on than thinking about matters of race all the time. I've recently discovered I like classical music. Down here in the boondocks, it's one of the only types of music available if you're not a fan of country and western. But I would feel like a damn fool studying classical music while half of my race is mired, and sinking deeper, into poverty. I would be as guilty as the young men I constantly upbraid about watching rap videos when they should be working on obtaining their GED.

There are many other areas of interest blacks have which they don't get to explore because of racism. You don't see blacks taking up the cause of, say, pollution of the environment, even though we are being poisoned by the same toxic fumes as everyone else, simply because racism keeps our noses too close to the civil-rights grindstone.

My most recent cellmate just went to the hole, and will probably get a disciplinary transfer, because he got into it with one of the easiest-going white hacks. Even all of the black convicts said my ex-cellie was way out of line. But the dude, who is pretty sharp otherwise, is so angry over racism, real or imagined, he is totally blinded. All he saw was that the guard was white. It can do that to you. The wonder is that even more minorities aren't pushed around the bend into madness.

A large percentage of black college students evidently feel the same way. Lately there has been concern expressed by college administrators over the tendency of the black students to self-segregate from their white counterparts. These middle-aged administrators feel their generation worked too hard, fought too many battles for equality, opened too many doors, for the black youth of the next generation to now allow these young people to segregate themselves. The black administrators especially feel this trend will be detrimental to both black and white youth in the long run, and they may be right.

However, I can sympathize with the black youth. The bloom is off the rose, so to speak, in terms of race relations. Many whites no longer go out of their way to make an isolated black feel comfortable. Maybe during the height of the Civil Rights movement this was true, but no longer. And many young blacks simply don't feel it's worth it to continue fighting the same battles we've been fighting for years without much success.

When other groups on college campuses, Asians, Latinos, and the like, choose to live in dormitories together, nothing is said. Not an eyebrow is raised. It is only when black students choose to do the same thing that it becomes a "problem."

Studies show that black students who live in all-black housing have a lower dropout rate and receive better grades than those who live in integrated housing. This shouldn't come as a surprise to anyone. They, like all other students, do better when they feel welcome and comfortable. For many of them it is their first time away from home. For some—those who attended all-black high schools—it is the first time they've been in proximity to whites for any length of time. While white administrators may go out of their way to make these students feel at home on campus, the majority of the white students are either unconcerned or hostile, just like in the real world. The socializing which goes on in college is part of developing "old boy" networks, and no matter how much young blacks attempt to integrate, they're never going to be part of those networks once their college days are over. It just doesn't happen.

What are young blacks to do, simply give up on integration? On a social level, yes. Go to the majority-white institutions, get an education, but realize America isn't really ready for true integration and conduct the remainder of your lives accordingly.

Some blacks will no doubt say that if we don't continue to keep banging our heads on the wall of institutionalized racism it will never fall. That this is the only way to dismantle it. My response is that we've pursued that course since World War II without making any real headway. Sure, things are better now for many blacks than they were then, but that has been due to the improvement in our economic condition, not to any success in terms of integration. Whatever prospering we have done has been in spite of institutional racism, not because it has reduced.

I repeat: the future of our race lies in self-determination, building racial pride and identity, not in integration.

SPIRITUALITY NEEDED

VIRTUALLY ANYONE who conquers a drug or alcohol problem does so through faith in a power higher than herself. This spirituality doesn't have to be of a particular brand: it can be Christian, Islam, Judaism, or one which goes by no name. Tom Robbins wrote something to that effect: "More people everyday are leaving organized religion and getting closer to God."

The overwhelming problems faced by the underclass of our country won't be solved until we find a method of awakening a sense of spirituality among these less fortunate souls.

The trouble, however, with many theisms is they often foster a belief—exclusively among poor people—that political and economic problems can be solved through prayer alone. Or worse, that the adherent should suffer his fate gladly since this suffering will put him in line for a bigger reward in some vague afterlife to come. While I have a strong belief in the power of spirituality, and attempt to keep my faith as pure as possible while remaining in submission to my own personal God, to accept mistreatment in the here and now for some later reward in some place which may or may not exist is sheer nonsense. You can keep any religion which has been perverted and then used in an attempt to keep me poor but happy.

My spirituality tells me that I am as good as any other of God's creatures and am therefore entitled to all of the bounty He supposedly provides for those who have and keep faith in Him. Here and now. Any problems I have with organized religion has nothing to do with spirituality, but with its past proclivity to bend to the will of, and be of assistance to, colonialists and those with imperialist leanings. Too often in history, the missionary has gone in first with his Bible to convince the natives to fall on their knees in supplication only to have the capitalists immediately follow and pick their collective pockets of whatever treasures the land might possess. All the while, the missionary tells the indigenous people that this is "God's will."

Martin Luther King Jr. once said "11 o'clock Sunday morning is the most segregated time in America." What gives organized religions a bad name among many minorities is the fact that most of those who loudly proclaim ours to be a "Christian nation," concerned with school prayer, family values, truth, justice, and the American Way, find it not the least bit difficult to reconcile their insincere incantations with overt racist behavior.

One aspect of national white schizophrenia is that they profess peace, love, and brotherhood while practicing hate, bigotry, and prejudice. The fiery cross of the Ku Klux Klan is still firmly burned into the consciousness of many black and other minority Americans. The fact that now the racism is dressed in different robes, manifested in different ways, and carried out with a veneer of civility while being protected by specious laws which give a patina of justice to the slow genocide being systematically practiced against the black and brown races is not lost on the underclasses.

One of the more regularly used cop-outs by adherents of different religions is that their particular sect shouldn't be castigated because of the failings of some of its believers, and they're right. Virtually all religions are perfectly conceived and written. If their strictures and scriptures were followed, even loosely, we would have something close to a utopian world. The present state of the planet, with all of the war, famine, and upheaval, is testament to how far most people have strayed from the teachings of their chosen religions.

For a religion to be followed by a group of people, that religion has to fulfill some basic needs of those people. Look into our nation's ghettos. Is it any wonder there is a lack of spirituality to be found in these pockets of despair? What blacks have to learn is how to renew their faith in God, increase their spirituality, while ignoring the religions that have failed them so miserably. For years they put their faith and belief in a better tomorrow in the hands of church-led civil-rights organizations only to see their condition steadily decline.

If any representatives of any of the world's major religions were to demonstrate that they are ready and willing to live by the tenets of their faith and use the power of their organization to uplift these downtrodden, I think you would witness the inhabitants of the ghettos flocking to that religion in droves. However, since these poor folk won't be able to enrich any church until their problems of poverty and unemployment are effectively dealt with, I don't think you'll see any ministers rushing in to fill poor folks' spiritual needs.

When the time has come for the underclass, after first learning to minister to their own spiritual needs, to come together under one religion or spiritual banner, God, in His infinite wisdom, will make it known to them.

QUIT LAUGHING!

RECENTLY A NUMBER of white television critics have decried the language used by black comedians on programs such as *Def Comedy Jam* and others of this ilk. They see the constant use of the word "bitch" as being derogatory towards women in general and black women in particular. These critics certainly have a lot of company among older blacks who are also upset with this trend of language. I can, to some degree, understand how they feel about the use of the word since I have a word of my own which makes me cringe whenever I hear it. And around this prison I hear it quite a lot: nigger.

No, it's not some white racist saying it; it's one young black saying it to another, and sometimes in front of white racists. They'll use it anywhere and everywhere. But does the fact that it makes me cringe make their usage of it wrong? Probably not. Lenny Bruce used to go on stage and say "niggerniggerniggerniggernigger." It was his way of saying that if a harmful word was repeated it lost its ability to harm.

These young blacks don't mean to disrespect each other when they call each other nigger; it's just part of their speech, whether I like or am comfortable with it or not. Let one of the white guys call them a nigger and watch out!

It's much the same with the black language being heard on cable-television comedy programs. It seems the whites (and older middle-class blacks) are disturbed by the use of words which they don't approve of. Should these youths deny part of their culture—yes, I said *their* culture!— because it upsets someone else? I fully realize that language is the first step in developing an attitude which accepts degradation toward women, and we certainly hear enough rap lyrics which do that. But the two shouldn't be confused. Every use of the word *bitch* isn't meant to be degrading. The rap lyrics are offensive because they make sex objects of women and glorify violence. The use of the word *bitch* doesn't necessarily connote all of that, no matter how much misunderstanding whites might think that it does.

I've played both sides of the fence, so to speak, and on the down side of black life the word *bitch* is used interchangeably with the word woman. Such as, "I've got the best bitch in the world." And a black woman who is up on this form of argot takes this for what it is: a compliment. It's a black thang.

I would imagine these white critics (and their black supporters) would feel more comfortable if these black comedians would tell political jokes rather than focus so much on graphic sexual material. I know I enjoy the comics who speak to contemporary social issues much more than those who simply find new ways to describe the sex act and female genitalia. I find them somewhat lacking in talent. But laughter is so important I'm willing to set aside my queasiness about the material as long as it provides a laugh. The black race sorely needs as much of the enlightening freedom laughter supplies as it can get.

As we become more aware of political situations we, as a race, will find more humor in political jokes. Does this mean we shouldn't (or don't deserve to) laugh until we all find the same things humorous? Maybe part of the problem is jealousy. These critics, who as part of their jobs, must watch some of these freewheeling black comedy programs, feel left out. They just don't get it, which is understandable since they don't have the frame of reference to be able to see the humor in the material. Again, does that make it less significant than political humor, at least to the black audiences? To the white critics maybe it does, but that fact certainly can be viewed as elitist, if not racist. We don't need whites' approval to laugh, nor do we need them telling us what to laugh at.

The first time I called my current woman *bitch* she got upset. So I apologized and told her I didn't know the word upset her so. I hadn't realized how square she was. Then I told her, "Look bitch, you'd better get used to it since I'm too old to change. And every woman in the world is a bitch except your mother and my mother!" Now she is much happier since she now has the right to call me some things she's always wanted to call a man, and which sometimes accurately describe my behavior. Does it mean we respect each other any less than people who don't refer to each other with such language? Of course not. We are each other's everything. Sometimes she's my woman and sometimes she's my bitch. And sometimes she's just a plain bitch. Like I said, it's a black thang.

IN DEFENSE OF
SOMETHING I DETEST

THE NATIONAL CONGRESS of Black Women has targeted hardcore "gang-sta" rap because of the disturbing message it carries to young people. The fact that most of the records are bought by white youths not black youths is little solace for these black women and, if anything, highlights rap's ability to infect youth of all cultures.

Not satisfied with producing a repetitious beat and hard-to-comprehend (to my mind), nonsensical lyrics, the form has gone on to develop into the most misogynistic garbage ever recorded. Its debasement of females is made all the more complete when one sees young black women fiercely shaking their rumps on the videos, giving, by their participation, tacit approval.

It is easy to understand these young women's excitement at being seen in a video, but it is a sad commentary on how we've raised them that they willingly allow themselves to be so used and, evidently unknown to them, abused.

This form of self-hatred by young blacks attempts to excuse itself by proclaiming it only reflects the realities of the ghetto. However, since one can reasonably argue that life often imitates art, this pernicious form of music can, and does, lead young people to attempt to emulate the lifestyles they see portrayed on the videos, violence and all. Throughout history, it has been known that teenagers can be a particularly vicious lot, without the encouragement of rap videos.

It is now well documented that most sex deviants are found to be addicted to hardcore pornography, which gives ample reason to speculate it will not be long before a similar connection will be made between rap videos and ghetto violence, if it hasn't already been made. Even if there isn't a connection to be made, the proud display of ignorance on the part of some rappers is reason enough to wish the industry would clean up its act. The last thing our youths need is exposure to more garbage in their lives.

However, in spite of all of this, I would be loath to support the National Congress of Black Women in its efforts to have rap banned from the shelves of music stores. I would gladly support a boycott, or even picketing in an attempt to dissuade people from purchasing the music. But an outright ban, no. Yes, you guessed it. It's that nettlesome old First Amendment again.

While I could support efforts to regulate, via the FCC, what goes out over the airwaves (albeit somewhat reluctantly) I can't, no matter how much I detest rap, go along with efforts to muzzle artists. Even categorizing these purveyors of filth as "artists" is difficult enough for me to do, since that puts them in the same class as serious musicians. I've long felt one of the main reasons for rap's popularity is the fact that much of it it is so simple many can perform it with minimal talent or training. Thus, young people who are not seven feet tall or have the ability to perform amazing feats with some kind of ball can cling to the dream they too can use rap as a vehicle out of the ghetto. Maybe this is justification enough to let youth have its day. Who knows, maybe the music will eventually turn into something. After all, our parents hated our music, too.

A stronger reason not to support these fine women is that I don't like wasted effort. While their attempt will make these women feel they are indeed doing something worthwhile, the net results will come to nil. The First Amendment is too sacrosanct to be tampered with because of some group's likes or dislikes.

Rapping started in prison, thus the strong beat with little else behind the performers. In jail, with no access to musical instruments, the young convicts made do and expressed their rage at a system which they felt unfairly incarcerated them. This somewhat understandable sentiment soon, however, degenerated into a form of hatred for anything or anyone who ever had control over their lives, thus the evolution of misogynistic lyrics. Many of the young women they rap about have precious little to use to control anything in their lives (including these young men) but their sexuality, and some of them learn to use it like a weapon. This however, could, prove to be the key to curtailing the nastier side of rap.

The members of the National Congress of Black Women should use its influence with the young girls who appear in the videos and buy the rap records and tapes. If it was able to convince the girls to boycott performers who disrespect women, and to refuse to appear in the videos or buy the tapes, as well as to date or speak to these young men, I guarantee you this would lead to a very sudden death for the "gangsta."

Scoring Some Points That Count

WHETHER WE WISH to realize it or not, our black superstar athletes have more influence on our black youths as role models and opinion shapers than Jesse Jackson, Douglas Wilder, and the dynamic new junior senator from Illinois, Carol Moseley Braun, all rolled into one. And this influence extends not just to youngsters of the underclass but middle-class black youths and adults, also.

One fairly recent phenomenon of black culture is the ascendancy of youthful opinion in determining matters of mores and lifestyles within our race. Whereas in years gone by the opinions of paterfamilias set the tenor and tone of acceptable behavior for black youth, our youths now perform this task for themselves. And they set liberal boundaries indeed, as readily evidenced by the now-routine teenage pregnancies which no longer raise an eyebrow.

To be fair, I have to state this behavior is indicative of the times and not wholly exclusive to black culture. White kids are running amok, too. But since their culture is more firmly established—in terms of being stronger financially—white youths have a farther height to fall from (and larger cushions to catch them) before doing irreparable damage to their lives and family structures.

As our black youths have witnessed, their parents become bitter from struggling against poverty and racism, only to see whatever meager gains made quickly wiped out. They begin to doubt their parents' potency, which in turn leads to disrespect for their authority. And nothing can be as bitterly challenging as a fifteen year old.

Since these youths rarely read newspapers or news magazines, the only blacks they see winning (other than the neighborhood dope dealer) are athletes. And even when these superstars lose, idolizing youth know they still, at the end of the game, slide into the seat of a $100,000-plus vehicle and ride off into the sunset, usually accompanied by a gorgeous woman.

We have about as much chance of loosening the sway these black demi-gods hold over black youth as we do of electing a black president. Better we attempt to convince these young millionaires of the responsibility they have to their race, which won't be easy. While some of the professional athletes already have a social conscience and attempt to give something back to the community and their race, many more of them are simply overgrown spoiled brats. The white system which turns them into pampered and callous individuals evidently tells them to avoid saying or doing anything which may assist their own race.

The reigning superstar of basketball, now that Michael Jordan has retired, went out of his way to announce he "was nobody's role model." As if he has a choice in the matter. It goes with the millions, you idiot. Sure, parents are supposed to be the role models, but many of these young men rarely see someone they call father, some not at all. These children are going to attempt to emulate their favorite athletes whether they like it or not. What would it really cost these young men to make an effort to reach back and help their own race? Not much.

Now I don't expect these young millionaires to become Goody Two-shoes. It would be almost un-American if they didn't go out and raise a little hell every now and then; that goes with the millions, too. However, no matter how insulated they are from the grinding poverty of the ghettos (the same ghettos many of them came from) they still should make room on their agendas to do what they can for their race. And they can do plenty.

Virtually any program they wholeheartedly endorse will catch on with the public. There is a crying need for grass-roots activism and volunteerism within the black community. Look at the efforts of former football great Jim Brown.

From drugs to gang violence to teen pregnancies, the only solutions are going to have to come from within the black communities. And no one is better positioned to lead this much-needed wave of black involvement than black athletes. I'm not asking for their money, just their time and commitment, and their inspiration. I'm asking them to go out into the communities and let the people see them getting involved. The people will come out. It matters little if the people first come out simply to see the superstar. They'll get involved because the project has his seal of approval.

What right do I, or anyone else, have making demands on these professional athletes' time? All the right in the world. We are members of the same black race, and if that doesn't mean anything to them, I'm left to wonder what they learned in college. They have a *duty* to help. And they should be proud to be in a position to be able to do so.

EMPTY BLACK SOUND BITES

OFTENTIMES, WHEN WATCHING black entertainers on talk or awards shows as they make what to them is a heartfelt plea to black youths of the ghetto to disavow violence, I wonder what is going through their minds. I don't like to impugn these fellow blacks' sincerity, or categorize their efforts as simple self-serving aggrandizement at the expense of less privileged blacks, but I still am left to wonder.

Watching them pretend to themselves and the audience that their fame and wealth afford them influence and power with disenfranchised youth makes me want to laugh. I find it hard to believe these clucks actually think case-hardened gangbangers are going to take heed of their admonishments. Like the dumb anti-drug commercials which blare "Don't Do Drugs," but nothing else, these sound bites from superstar blacks are incomplete messages. Would that it were so easy as simply telling these youths what they shouldn't be doing, any fool can do that. The hard part, and what the black entertainers, and the commercials too for that matter, don't do is tell them what they should be doing instead. That, of course, would take longer than thirty seconds, which is about all the time these guys seem willing to devote to the problem.

Just as nature abhors a vacuum, for these youngsters to give up what they have, what they know about, and in all probability have been doing for years, and not replace it with something else is impossible. They are not just going to sit in their project apartments and stare at the four walls. The vast majority of them know they are doing wrong, but at least they are doing something, their thinking goes. Breaking bad habits which took years to acquire will take more than just some rich black dude pleading with them to stop.

What these black entertainers are doing (besides making themselves feel good at someone else's expense) is acknowledging that they know there is a serious problem out there. They'd better quit doing this or some-one will call their bluff and ask them to *really* do something other than make wind in public.

They probably are attempting to expiate their guilt over not really doing anything to help the less fortunate of their own race. Or they could be attempting to increase their stature within the black community and thereby increase the ratings of whatever career vehicle they happen to be working on at the moment. You never know with these people, most entertainers are a selfish and slippery lot at best.

The old stories, put out by their handlers and flunkies, about how much they are doing behind the scenes without taking any credit, are soon going to have a harder time flying. The situation in our nation's ghettos is reaching critical mass, and discrete, covert efforts are *not* going to cut it. Something substantive and public needs to be done, and done soon.

And I'm not referring to some hands-off fund-raiser where everyone stands around nibbling Brie, sipping champagne, and decrying how bad "those people" have it. Other than add lustre to the entertainer's image and get their picture in a magazine, the only outcome of these events is sponsorship for an already upwardly mobile young black who probably would have received a scholarship to college anyway.

Everyone loves to help a winner, and we blacks are no exception. We do a damn good job of helping those of our race who least need it. Not that we don't need more black lawyers and CPAs, we do. But the real crying need is from the child in the ghetto who won't make it out of high school without positive intervention of a personal nature.

These blessed entertainers need to do more than just talk. While most of them probably haven't seen a ghetto in years—unless they were one of the "influential stars" trotted out by the establishment during the L.A. riots—someone should inform them that the ghettos are still there and the problems are greater than ever.

They could do many good things if they were so inclined. Jim Brown has demonstrated how much difference one person can make. Imagine if dozens more were following his lead. It could make a substantial differ-ence to a lot of youth.

Black entertainers are the closest thing the black race has to royalty. They are idolized, worshipped, and the source of great pride for many of us. But just as royalty has its privileges it also has its responsibilities and obligations, ones that can't be discharged with lip service alone. It's time for them to actually do something, or shut the hell up.

HATEFUL RHETORIC

THE RECENT FLAP over the speech a minister of the Nation of Islam, the religious organization headed by Louis Farrakhan, made at a New Jersey college brings to light a long-smoldering issue between blacks and Jews, as well as within the black community itself.

The fact the racist and anti-Semitic statements were far out of line and are now being condemned by many blacks is excellent proof not all, nor even the majority, of blacks approve of this type of rhetoric.

There has undeniably been friction between the two groups over the last twenty years. That the two groups can't seem to work their differences out and move forward together in their efforts to confront a common enemy is sad. The same racist who will burn a cross one night will paint a swastika on a synagogue the next.

The type of demagoguery engaged in by members of the Nation of Islam needs to be combatted by all right-thinking people, no matter their race or color. It wasn't too many years ago, another demagogue in Germany used a similar approach to eventually justify his "final solution." Why the ministers of the Nation of Islam can't see that by their racist attacks on Jews they are aiding in creating an atmosphere where such attacks are acceptable is unfathomable. If that is accomplished, it is no mean guess as to which group will be next to be attacked. He who lives by the sword of bigotry, dies by the sword of bigotry.

After the statements in this case are firmly rebuked, those religious leaders and others who have expressed so much concern about them should then turn their efforts to the question of *why* such poisonous cant finds fertile soil and takes root in the minds of black college students. Supposedly the mostly black audience at the college cheered the speech. This should be as distressing as the speech itself.

What the minister of the Nation of Islam was taking advantage of is a newly awakened feeling among educated, and those seeking to become educated, blacks that there is something very wrong with what they've been taught in history books about themselves. Unfortunately, in too many cases, the dichotomy between what actually happened and what is written in Eurocentric textbooks concerning black history has been startling.

Now that these young people are discovering the truth, they are understandably angry. The fact that they are is very healthy. To become upset with racist versions of history will inspire them to discover what really happened after Africa was colonized and blacks were brought to the Americas. This information will give them a much-needed sense of identity, which in turn will build racial pride. The truth makes you free.

What I don't, and can't, agree with is what some people want to do with this knowledge. To use it to preach hate is counterproductive to the education process. History can't be rewritten. What happened happened. The reason blacks need to study their accurate past is so they can thereby be better equipped to deal with the problems of today, problems that were created by those past mistakes. History, however, shouldn't be used to create a generation of hatemongers and bigots.

What the mainstream black Christian leaders have to ask themselves is, could they have done something to better address the frustration felt by the disaffected black youth who cheer hate speeches? Could the leaders have, along with giving them a religious foundation, introduced them, in a nonhateful manner, to the sins and crimes which were committed against the black race?

There is evidently a void to be filled in these students' lives and feelings in regard to these matters or the words of hate spewed forth by the minister of the Nation of Islam would not have found willing ears. Whoever effectively and honestly addresses the issues and feelings created by the new consciousness, inspired by better education of young blacks will, in large part, determine how well this education is used. So far, the field has been left completely open to the haters and distorters of the Nation of Islam. They have honed their skills in capturing youthful black minds and imaginations in our nation's prisons, and are now moving on to colleges. How long other religious groups, including mainstream Muslims, will allow this to continue unchallenged is anyone's guess.

DOWN AND DIRTY WITH THE MINISTER

I TRY TO FOLLOW the dictum of never speaking ill of another black but am forced to break that rule in the case of Louis Farrakhan.

For some time now, the mindless, hateful rhetoric he and his followers venomously spew forth has caused me, as well as many other serious-minded blacks, a lot of concern. What tipped the scales against him for me personally was a series of occurrences in the Washington, D.C., area a few years ago. I wasn't aware until recently of the clinics The Nation of Islam had set up to bilk AIDS-infected people with a fraudulent "cure." The transcripts of the incident, which was featured on *Primetime*, were enough to push me around the bend. The man is a mountebank, a fraud, and a pimp.

He has taken the legitimate concerns, fears, and aspirations of a whole race of people and carelessly turned them to his advantage, financial and otherwise.

He and his "religion" turned from hatred of all whites to focus mainly on Jews simply because someone in the Middle East is probably paying him to do so. Red herrings have often been used in the past by others to divert or distract adversaries, but in this case Farrakhan is manipulating his followers and other blacks without them gaining any of the benefits.

I could almost condone a scenario in which rich Arabs financially assisted American blacks in return for their support. That would be politics. Dirty politics to be sure, but then virtually all politics are dirty. But if any benefits are accruing, and I believe they are, Farrakhan is keeping them all for himself and his inner circle of followers. Which is not surprising; like I said, the man is a pimp.

The national black leadership, both religious and secular, has to assume responsibility for Farrakhan's rise to power. If it had provided reasonable militant leadership (yes, there can be such a thing) to the millions of blacks who have felt disfranchised for years, Farrakhan wouldn't have been able to gain the ear of so many of the discontented. These minds and bodies were forfeited to him via a leadership vaccum. Middle-class blacks, by ignoring the cries from our nation's ghettos, failed to field a team. No one was addressing the needs of this segment of the black population. He gave a voice to those who had none.

Prison inmates, drug abusers, and others who neither the white establishment nor middle-class blacks had any use or tolerance for have been welded into a powerful organization by The Nation of Islam. With their doctrines of clean living, abstention from alcohol and tobacco, self-sufficiency, and dedication to family, there can be no doubt The Nation has been a positive force in the lives of many.

But Farrakhan, like many another egotistical demagogues before him, has taken a legitimate premise and used it to justify illegitimate actions. And he has the perfect cover for those actions. Anyone who dares to raise his voice in opposition is branded either a racist (if he is white) or an Uncle Tom (if he happens to be black). Farrakhan creates and maintains a siege mentality expressly for the purpose of hiding behind the mantle of a leader whites wish to oppress. My writing this would no doubt qualify me for the latter category of Uncle Tom. However, if one considers my life, my struggles, and the whole of the body of my writings, any such attempt to smear my reputation will be discounted by any reasonable individual. Naturally, Farrakhan's followers will believe it, but then they'll believe anything.

One of the prime tenets of The Nation is an absolute blindness and suspension of reasoning powers on the part of adherents. They have to swallow whatever cock and bull story he feeds them hook, line, and sinker, and of course Farrakhan's hiding behind the title of "oppressed leader" cheapens that label in the eyes of those opposed to black gains.

All religions have certain strongly held beliefs on which they are based, and many of those beliefs, at least to nonmembers, might seem strange. But this is what religious tolerance is all about; you can believe in and pray to a rock for all I care. That's *your* business. However, when a religious group purposely engenders public controversy by spewing forth hate as The Nation has, then its basic beliefs have a right to be called into question, if for no other reason than to try to determine where the reckless rhetoric is emanating from.

Many young blacks—due in part to the popularity of the film *Malcolm X*—are beginning to listen to Minister Farrakhan. It empowers them to hear someone ridicule, casitgate, and vilify white folks. The public meetings which The Nation has been holding on college campuses around the country are truly rabble-rousing in nature. They give frustrated young blacks a chance to publicly (some for the first time in their lives) vent their pent-up frustrations. Maybe this is justification enough for these young people to attend.

But this is the future of our black race Farrakhan and his followers are so callously tinkering with and manipulating here. He'd better tread carefully. Damn carefully.

MAKING A BAD TRADE

ISLAM IS THE FASTEST-GROWING RELIGION in the United States, with more than 4 million followers, one-third of whom are African-Americans. Somewhere between 50,000 and 100,000 are followers of the Louis Farrakhan-led Nation of Islam.

Founded by an itinerant Russo-Syrian silk peddler named W. Fard in Detroit in 1930, The Nation of Islam, under the leadership of Elijah Mohammad, first experienced spectacular growth during the sixties, due mainly to the efforts of its charismatic roving minister Malcolm X.

The Nation, as it is known to its followers, recruits heavily among prison inmates, taking young black men and giving them a sense of belonging, identity, and purpose they have never before known. Former drunkards, addicts, and wife-abusers are transformed, as if by magic, into men with devout religious beliefs, a strong sense of family, and extraordinary discipline.

Many now believe The Nation of Islam is the only organization which has the power, reputation, and dedication to bring order to the chaos which currently reigns in our nation's ghettos. Based on my experiences with converted Muslims I would have to concur. Many young blacks are attracted to the strong rhetoric of Louis Farrakhan. Considering the degree of racism most of them encounter, and the failing of other efforts to effectively combat it, there is little reason to wonder why the minister's message is attractive to these disfranchised youths.

Martin Luther King Jr.'s uplifting message of Christian reconciliation has had little ongoing effect on our struggle for social justice and racial equality. Since, by many measures, we, as a race, are worse off than we were in the sixties, many young blacks are ready to try another approach. The failing of the olive branch of brotherhood has led some to place their faith in the savage power of the avenging Muslim sword.

Personally I feel we make a great mistake when we unite behind any religious leader or banner to seek racial justice. Trading our faith in the power of one religion to bring us equality for faith in another is foolhardy.

By doing so we are attacking the problem with the wrong means. Our founding fathers distinctly separated church and state for very good reason. They meant for one to not be able to affect the other, for the good of both. One ministers to man's soul, the other concerns itself with temporal affairs. Try as we might, we'll never pray our way in a good Christian manner to full equality, nor will we achieve it by predicting the doom of the white race and the "lifting of the so-called black man up to his rightful place."

The dangers of following a charismatic religious leader—no matter what brand of religion he espouses—are inherent, and they should, by now, be obvious. Charismatic personalities rarely are interested in building a strong organization to leave behind. Indeed, often *they* are the organization. Upon their demise, untimely or otherwise, the followers flounder leaderlessly about waiting for the next Messiah-like figure to point the way towards the Promised Land.

Historically, the black church has been the strongest organization within the black community and therefore became by default the organization we used to achieve equality. However, the contribution made by the church shouldn't be denigrated. Our religious leaders accomplished near miracles under sometimes near-impossible conditions.

However, the time has now come for blacks to form an organization which is purely political, an NAACP with some spit and fire to it. A vehicle designed expressly for our purposes will stand a much better chance of successfully addressing what are basically political problems than a religious organization can. We cannot overcome institutionalized racism by praying in front of a cross or bumping our heads on the floor five times a day.

What good does it do us to give up our faith in solving our problems by believing in fantastic miracles, such as virgin births and resurrections, only to trade them in for stories about motherships hovering above us somewhere, dispatching messages to earth through Muslim ministers?

We need religion in our lives. It can lead to the salvation of our souls. We need organized political activism in our lives also. It can lead us out of the wilderness of economic and racial oppression. But we have to keep the two of them distinctly separate in our minds if we are to utilize either of them to their optimum success potential.

GOD DON'T LIKE UGLY

THE RELIGION OF CHOICE for black prison inmates is fast becoming Islam. More and more, those convicts who choose to embrace any religion at all follow one of the three Muslim faiths now popular in America: The Nation of Islam; The Moorish Science Temples of America, Inc., founded in the twenties by Noble Drew Ali; and the Sunni Muslims, who follow a more traditional brand of the religion imported from the Middle East.

The fact that many blacks, even some of those who followed Christianity when they entered prison, are turning toward "the true religion of the black man" should come as a surprise to no one. Even before the popularity of the Spike Lee film *Malcolm X*, many young blacks found the strong rhetoric of the more militant Muslim sects appealing. Couple this strong talk with a teaching of history of the black man which is entirely different from what they were exposed to in school and the reason the sect is growing so fast becomes obvious. In addition to teaching pride, it teaches respect and discipline.

The converts figure it just makes more sense to pray to a God of their own skin color than the white Son of God hanging on a cross. When one stops to consider that virtually every race or nationality of people who prays to a god of another race or skin color is poor, arguments against these young men embracing Islam don't seem logical.

While I personally risk my soul to perdition and damnation by not embracing any organized religion (to me they are, no matter what the followers say, all the same and comparing them is like comparing different brands of washing detergents; any of them will cleanse the soul if used properly) and yet feel comfortable with the followers of any, I suppose if I were to participate in organized religion it would be as a Muslim. The fact that I don't probably has more to do with the fact that I'm not an "organizational person," having been kicked out of the Cub Scouts at age seven for rules infractions, than with anything else. Like Groucho Marx quipped, "I wouldn't want to join any group that would have *me* as a member."

While I attempt to constantly stay in submission to my God, much to the consternation of some religious people who say I can't be successful without attending a formal church, I continue to feel I don't need a middleman to keep me in touch with my God. I've found, over the years, reading from the world's great religions to be very inspirational. I can still find words of solace and comfort in any of them. It is only when I read or hear about the interpretations put on the various religions by modern-day clerics do I usually find something which sticks in my craw. When the follower of one brand states theirs to be the only true brand, they quickly lose me. I can't imagine a heaven with only Christians, or Jews, or only Muslims, for that matter.

Also situations like Northern Ireland, Bosnia, and the Middle East— and all of the other millions of people who have died over the centuries in the name of religion—leave me cold.

The fact is, all too often the followers of different brands of religions can't seem to wait to castigate followers of another brand. A good example occurred recently here at the prison. Muslims are treated like they are second-class citizens in the eyes of the Lord by the priest who runs the chapel. I wrote a skit to celebrate Kwanzaa, and a friend who is Muslim repeatedly asked the chaplain for chapel time so we could put on a program celebrating black-history month, which the skit in question was to be part of. This supposedly religious man hemmed and hawed about granting permission until Kwanzaa had passed, and then came up with a lame excuse that, try as he might, he just couldn't fit it into the schedule of the chapel, even though two groups who have time set aside each week were willing to let us use it. Incidents like this are routine, at least at this prison.

I know, I know, I shouldn't make judgments about a religion based on the actions of one man, but the lack of respect Muslims receive for simply following their faith is shameful. This type of treatment is too allopatric to be incidental. A pattern throughout America is too easily detectable.

I firmly believe there is a God. And, as Nietzsche once said, "If God didn't exist man would have to invent Him." But I know in my heart He does exist, and, like my mother used to say, "God don't like ugly."

PAPER TIGERS

PRISON IS FILLED with tough young men who know how to walk that walk and talk that talk. To listen to them they are the baddest dudes to come out of the ghetto since *Superfly.* They flash all the gang signs, wear the colors, and brag about being "O.G.," Original Gangsters.

On the street they showed no mercy as they turned their own neighborhoods into killing fields battling over "turf," which more than likely actually belongs to some white, suburban, absentee slumlord than to them or their ancestors.

They crowd into the television room to listen in rapt attention to rap songs with inane lyrics which glorify violence and killing while denigrating their mothers, sisters, and bearers of their own offspring. This they argue is an "art form." Like everyone else, they love to see images of themselves and their former lifestyles portrayed on film and you can hear a pin drop as they watch movies which show inner-city youths mowing each other down like so many bowling pins. They can identify all of the different weapons of destruction from a distance and love to discuss the relative merits of the various guns as they brag about how many people they blew away, often simply because they were "dissed."

They inflate their own egos with their argot; when one of their "road dogs" asks them how they are doing they proudly reply "just chillin' like a villain."

They excuse their lifestyles, with all of its attendant violence, killing, and infecting of their own neighborhoods with drugs by posturing as some kind of "black liberators" who are actually fighting "racist oppression" by their mindless acts of cruelty.

They wear their prison sentences as badges of honor. Indeed, to them going to prison is no more than a rite of passage. The more time they've done the more respect they find among their peers since they are viewed as "hardcore."

But something is out of focus here. All of this tough talk just doesn't add up. If these dudes are so tough why then are they in prison? Why didn't they, upon being accosted by the police, just whip out their trusty Mac-10s and shoot their way out of the situation? I mean, these guys are proven killers, right? According to them (and police departments across the country) they were better equipped than some small armies. They all have photo albums which are chock full of pictures sent in from the street with them proudly displaying their weaponry. And they certainly don't place a high value on human life (even their own according to them) as the tear drops tattooed under their eyes (which signify how many men they've supposedly killed) attest to.

My question is, when the police roll up on them why is it you see nothing but hands thrust out of windows as they attempt to grab a piece of the sky? They know full well what's in store for them. They've seen the Rodney King tapes. The cops are, at minimum, going to spread-eagle them on the ground like a bear rug and *really* do some dissing, calling them all sorts of punks and faggots and daring them to peep a reply.

Why didn't these tough dudes, instead of attempting to hide their guns under the seat of the car, throw down on the rollers?

Could it be that the police aren't helpless and the defenseless youths were on their way home from trying to obtain an education? Could it be because they know the police will shoot back that they didn't bust off a few caps in their direction as they made a daring getaway?

Or could it be that most of these lost, overgrown children are just paper tigers, not as willing to be killed as they are to kill? You see, that's the difference between real bad dudes and these man-children I see around me everyday: real bad guys are just as willing to die as they are to kill. These dudes aren't.

So they can stuff all of the rhetoric; try to impress someone who doesn't know any better. All of the real tough dudes are in the cemetery, not sitting around prison bragging about how tough they are. Those who actually live by the code of death and destruction eventually die by the same code. They don't live to brag about it.

However, in spite of these youths' demeanor and how much they aggravate me with their overblown and distorted senses of reality, they are still my little brothers, and God knows they didn't raise themselves to be the way they are. They are the product of a society in which racism purposely causes them to fail. Most of them had very few options.

Don't Follow the Leader

Black history in America is filled with courageous men and women who risked life and limb to advance the causes of the race. From Nat Turner, Harriet Tubman, and Frederick Douglass, through W.E.B. DuBois and Marcus Garvey, to Adam Clayton Powell, Rosa Parks, Malcolm X, and Dr. Martin Luther King Jr., to Jesse Jackson and Louis Farrakhan, many men and women have sought to lead the race, or in some cases had the mantle of leadership thrust upon them, to a better tomorrow.

Ours is an oral culture. From the proverbs of African tribe elders to our most eloquent spokespersons of today we have been moved, inspired, and roused by silver-tongued orators. We have, in large part, selected our leaders based on their ability to communicate with us via the spoken word. The fact that our black ministers are most masterly in this method of communication has caused them to often be in the forefront of our struggles. And our leaders, both in and out of the clergy, have always responded to our adulation and needs with inspired leadership.

If there has been any drawback to our method of selecting leaders to advance the causes of the race, it has been that too often when the leader is removed, often by violent death, from our midst the movement stalls, sputters, and is often set back. This can be said about any organization, no matter the race of the members, which is lead by a charismatic leader. This phenomenon certainly isn't limited to the black race.

However, since our leaders tend to rise up out of the necessity of the times rather than through a political process—the method whereby most white leaders are selected—our progress has been much more dependent on one gifted person rather than an established leadership selection process. I mean in no way to denigrate the leadership our race has had in the past, but our future is too important to trust to such a haphazard method of selecting our leaders in the future. Times are becoming much too complex.

239

The fact is we need a broader vision than only one person can provide. We need leadership by an ongoing committee of the best minds within the race, regardless of their membership in black or civil-rights organizations. As matters currently stand our best people aren't solicited for the positions of advisers to the race, quite the opposite. Those who think they have the answers (and often have a hidden agenda) to our problems and have an organization and a decent speaking voice become our spokesmen, regardless as to whether they have the right answers or not.

Often these self-styled leaders do in fact have the right solution, or at least part of it. That still leaves us with the problem of the vacuum which could be created upon their untimely demise. Often men of this temperament fail to bring along anyone to take over their position and keep the organization on track in the event something happens, which limits their ability to be able to finish their work.

To a degree, we've solved the problem by launching *Emerge*, a national magazine which focuses on current black issues. Without a means of the race staying on the same page, so to speak, in regard to the issues we would be forever doomed to trust the white media to define our problems and concerns for us. Now it becomes imperative for the most gifted of our race to formulate a far-sighted strategy which can get us from where we are today to where we need to be five, ten, twenty years down the road. Not to start such a group leaves us at the mercy of any black demagogue who comes along with a twisted message, one that sounds to the uneducated ear like gospel. Our wise black thinkers cannot afford to abandon the field to mere cant and hollow rhetoric.

Our youths are desperately seeking answers. The old ways of gradualism no longer hold validity for them. They say, if we are indeed due these rights, why do we have to wait for them to be parcelled out to us? If indeed, they *are* ours and we are entitled to all of them right now, not in some distant tomorrow which has been coming for the last 130 years and still has yet to arrive. We are so anxious to have our pernicious foe racism vanquished we will listen to anyone who arouses our sense of indignation. The constant delaying and putting off of our access to our full rights has created an anger in young black people which is not going to go away.

However, to allow someone to channel this anger into hatred of another group or race because of past real or imagined grievances, instead of using this energy to power positive change is foolhardy. It escapes me how positive change can come from negative hatred. I've found hatred always hurts the hater more than the hated in the long run.

Our race has been put upon, vilified, ostracized, and held back by many groups. Do we waste our effort and trivialize our cause by simply mouthing hatred against those who have done us injustice? If we do, we're going to miss our opportunity to improve our condition while we wallow in vindictive self-righteousness. Our cause is simply too noble; we mustn't let hate inspire us.

We certainly need to accurately study our history to determine how we were placed in the position we find ourselves in at present, and by whose hand. But then, armed with such knowledge we need to move forward to rectify the problems afflicting our race. And to do this we have to devise a method which will provide ongoing aggressive leadership. This is a job which is far too big and important for merely one leader.

EMERGE

A DISTURBING ARTICLE in *USA Today* (July 13, 1994) related the saddening news that if *Emerge*, the national black news magazine, doesn't receive an infusion of cash it is at risk of having to cease publication. I pray that by the time you read this the crisis will have passed and *Emerge* will be well on the road to being the healthy, viable publication concerned blacks so desperately need.

Emerge made its debut right before I was arrested, and I didn't become aware of its existence until it had been around for almost two years. It's ironic that I got my hands on a copy of the magazine on the same day I'd finished an essay decrying the need for just such a publication. The essay pointed out the supreme importance of all serious movements having an organ by which it keeps its followers on the same page, so to speak. The importance of disseminating information to a movement quickly and accurately can't be overstated. If the black-rights movement, dormant as it currently seems to be, is to ever become successful, it will be, in part, due to a magazine similar to *Emerge*.

It matters little if all blacks aren't like me, one who reads the magazine from cover to cover in one sitting. It matters even less that many blacks are still stuck reading only the black puff and fluff magazines which have been around for years (and have done very little to advance the cause of civil rights). The fact remains *Emerge* is a real necessity for black folks.

I've written to *Emerge* on a number of occasions. I've written a letter to the editor, an opinion for the Last Word column which features contributions from readers, and I've written to members of the executive staff. Sadly, I've never received a response of any sort, not even a postcard acknowledging receipt of my letters. This is not unusual for me since I make no secret of the fact in my correspondence that I'm an inmate at a federal prison. I've become accustomed to being completely ignored.

One of my letters (before I put my essays together for this book) was an attempt to interest *Emerge* in my work. Throughout the publication, I'd read stories about the shamefulness of the exceedingly high black incarceration rates and other expressions of outrage over how blacks are treated by the criminal-justice system. I thought the editors might be interested in the writings of someone who is actually on the *inside* and has first-hand experience. I obviously was wrong. Did I get my little feelings hurt? Damn right I did. I'd taken the time to craft my letters in a manner which I felt would demonstrate that I was a serious writer with worthwhile input. I took the editors' failure to respond as evidence of the black-middle-class propensity to be concerned about problems of the underclass only from a distance. These bourgeois blacks might want to help, I figured, as long as they didn't have to associate with the likes of me.

I admit I even spent a few delicious moments envisioning how I would snub them (along with many others) when I became famous for my work. Ha! Prison tends to cause such thoughts.

My bruised feelings aside, the fact is, blacks sorely need a publication of this type. I'm not completely happy with the hypocrisy of an article concerning the dangers of smoking juxtaposed by an ad for cigarettes, but since I'm aware of the realities of the magazine business, I can live with that. I also haven't wholeheartedly agreed with the point of view of some of the articles. But, by and large, they have done an excellent job of featuring issues which blacks should be, even if they aren't, concerned about. The decision to display Supreme Justice Clarence Thomas on one of its covers with a bandanna on his head, Aunt Jemima style, was courageous, and deadly accurate. The staff members, in other words, have been meeting their mission admirably.

When I was conceiving of a black news magazine, I envisioned a publication with no advertising at all. I felt the necessity of such a publication should inspire enough well-to-do blacks to provide funding for a foundation to cover the start-up expenses and allow it to exist by subscriptions only. This, I felt, would avoid the exact situation *Emerge* finds itself in at present. Magazine publishing is a very tough business, and given the fact that the American black population is only 10 percent, that many blacks simply aren't as involved in positive change for the race as they should be (a fact a magazine can overcome if given the precious commodity of time), and the costly process of publication, I knew any magazine for blacks would initially have a rocky road indeed. However, neither should these facts dissuade us from making the effort to keep such a publication afloat.

When Spike Lee ran into financial difficulties during the filming of *Malcolm X* (he was running behind schedule and over-budget, and the studio was threatening to withdraw its support) Magic Johnson, Oprah Winfrey, and a few other wealthy blacks acknowledged the importance of the film and bailed Mr. Lee out. A similar effort, if it comes to that, *must* be made for *Emerge*. Certainly there are enough blacks in America with the wherewithal to make such an investment.

If nothing is done and *Emerge* is allowed to cease publication I personally put a hex on every black millionaire in America. I imprecate them and name them for what they are: traitors to their own race. For too long now we have allowed those of our race who have the means, and a duty— yes! a *duty*—to stand idly by while our race flounders. This is no longer acceptable. We have to somehow prick the collective consciences of these members of our race. If it is left to me, yes me, a lowly criminal to do so, then so be it. For right is right, no matter who points it out. *We simply cannot allow* Emerge *to fail!*

A BRIGHTER TOMORROW

W.E.B. DuBois WROTE in 1906, in *The Souls of Black Folks*, "Progress in human affairs is more often a pull than a push, the surging forward of the exceptional man, and the lifting of his duller brethren slowly and painfully to his vantage-ground."

For a number of reasons the black middle class has been derelict in its duty to pull its less fortunate brethren along with it in its headlong rush to a brighter tomorrow. And, while I can intellectually and historically understand this failure, it doesn't make it any easier to accept.

During Reconstruction, blacks who clamored too loudly for their full rights were controlled by whites by lynchings, beatings, and imprisonment. With the assistance of Booker T. Washington (who, to his credit thought he was doing right) whites convinced other blacks to abandon these "belligerent niggers." If blacks wanted to be accepted by whites they had to be "good niggers." This attitude, to some degree, has persisted among American blacks—even though whites never kept their end of the bargain and never granted the rights they promised these blacks to this very day. Appeasement hasn't worked.

Blacks, by abandoning their less educated and poorer brethren, have lost the moral high ground. No race has ever advanced into the middle class piecemeal, with half moving ahead and the other half falling farther and farther behind. This abandonment of the underclass by better-off blacks has had two effects: one, it causes the covert proponents of institutionalized racism to adopt the attitude, "If you don't care about helping your poorer brethren I damn sure don't care!"; and two, it gave the world the impression our struggle wasn't so much about rights, as it was about financial gain for a select number of blacks.

When a black middle class began to develop after emancipation the only role models it had was the white bourgeoisie. And how did whites feel about poor blacks? Disdainful. So these first upwardly mobile blacks adopted this same attitude. After all, they reasoned, it was part of what made whites successful.

The same DuBois who wrote so eloquently about blacks at the turn of the century has to be castigated for his leadership of a faction within the black community that felt only lighter-skinned blacks should be granted the same rights as whites. The Niagara Movement (the forerunner of the NAACP, both of which DuBois was instrumental in founding) was notorious among darker-skinned blacks for instituting the "paper bag test." If an applicant wasn't as fairly complected as a brown paper bag she was denied entrance into the organization. While intraracial prejudice is a subject which makes many blacks uncomfortable, it has to be touched on, if for no other reason than it still, to some degree, exists among us. We have to purge ourselves of any vestiges of it before we can successfully move ahead.

When Marcus Garvey founded his Universal Negro Improvement Association in the early 1900s, its immediate and huge success was due largely to the fact that so many blacks had heretofore been denied membership in any other black-rights organization. However, Garvey's soaring popularity disturbed the blacks who had made championing black rights their personal domain, and they aggressively conspired with federal prosecutors to trump up charges to discredit and imprison Garvey, bringing to a quick close the best opportunity blacks had—and haven't had the equal of since—to improve their lot in America. Garvey, without a doubt, was potentially the most important man our race has ever produced.

Nothing much occurred for blacks in the area of civil rights during the remainder of the twenties since the great migration (the movement of blacks north to fill the jobs created by World War I) promised to solve all of our problems. During the thirties blacks were naturally the hardest hit by the Depression and whatever gains we had made or hoped for were lost as the nation attempted to recover from the catastrophic crash of '29.

Near the end of World War II black groups like the Tuskegee Airmen began to agitate for the integration of the armed forces. This set the stage for legal assaults against "separate but equal" education and Miss Rosa Parks's courageous and momentous decision that day on a Birmingham bus.

Never before in the history of the black race had anyone been more the right man, in the right place, at the right time than the Reverend Doctor Martin Luther King Jr. This giant's accomplishments still provide the main inspiration for the black civil-rights movement of today. Unfortunately for black Americans (and indeed all humankind) men like Dr. King come along only every few hundred years. The measure of his greatness lies in the fact that he was just beginning to expand his scope beyond the immediate problems of the black race to encompass other important social issues when he was killed. He rightly felt a man cannot limit himself to his own battles but must speak out against wrong whenever he encounters it. We would do well to heed that portion of his message today.

Blacks can no longer afford to be exclusive (if we ever could be) in our quest for our rights. We have to include the poor, the criminal, the entire underclass if we are to successfully address our myriad problems. Likewise we have to reach out to others outside of the black civil rights movement and assist them in addressing their concerns. It will do us little good to win full equality only to die from a poisoned environment.

It bears repeating: The same bigot who burns a cross one night will deface a synagogue the next, and bash a gay the night after.

Our wisest course is to raise a new generation of black leaders who are not confined by narrow self-interest but are emotionally, mentally, and spiritually prepared to lead us—all of us—to that brighter tomorrow.

A Time for Change

IN LIFE, TIMING IS EVERYTHING, or almost everything. The wisest, fairest, and most logical concept or plan can't be effectively put into motion and brought to successful fruition without proper timing.

However, timing is the one essential aspect of any equation over which potential implementers have the least amount of control or influence. Timing is directed by forces of history and circumstance which are beyond mere mortals' ability to control. When the timing is right the difficult becomes easy, the impossible possible, and the necessary accomplishable.

Such is now the case with the pervasive social problems of the now permanent underclass. The timing is right to address their problems in a manner which, once and for all, solves them. In the last 130 years, blacks have lurched from slavery to emancipation to Reconstruction to repression to benign neglect to civil-rights movements to white backlash to quotas and back again to benign neglect in their attempts to fit into the social fabric of America.

But now, at last, the confluence of politics, black-middle-class awareness, and heightened concerns of crime and violence (which is the by-product of maintaining a permanent underclass) have all provided the nation with its best opportunity yet to successfully address the problems. In politics, we now have a president who, while having compassion for the underclass and their problems, doesn't believe simply throwing money at them will lead to solutions.

The black middle class at last realizes no amount of education or hard work will guarantee career success in white corporate America and the only road to real success must be the one which lifts up the race as a whole. The conclusion they are making is that they, more than anyone else, are responsible for assuring that the one-third of their race mired in poverty doesn't remain there. Finally, and maybe most importantly, the continued downward spiral of the underclass has awakened the body politic to the fact that new methods have to be developed if we are serious about eliminating the pockets of poverty in this land of plenty. We are all suffering too much from the crime these conditions breed.

Government has to be willing to listen to those most affected by the problems of our inner cities and also be willing to lend a hand to blacks' efforts to lift up those of their race.

The ball is in the court of the black middle-class. The moral high ground in the struggle for full participation and equality in every aspect of American life can be seized and maintained only by insuring that our first priority is helping those of our race who have the least. Further advancing those who are already firmly in the middle-class is secondary. We have to come to the logical conclusion that no matter who is at fault for the present condition of the black underclass, it is mainly up to the rest of the black race to take the lead in solving its problems.

And the problems are indeed tough, so our solutions have to be tougher. Furthermore, most of these tough solutions will (and rightly so) have to be put forth by members of the black race, for if well-meaning whites were to propose them, cries of racism would reverberate throughout the land. The hard fact is that many of the methods which would adequately address the myriad problems of the underclass are, under any other circumstances, infringements on liberties. But circumstances in our nation's ghettos are far from normal. In fact, the only liberty which currently exists there is the right to die young.

Since the slums aren't going to disappear overnight we must, led by the black middle-class, rescue our black children from the mean streets and neighborhoods. Starting with those still in the wombs of teenaged mothers, and moving up the age ladder as quickly as possible and as far as necessary, for those children most at risk of being mentally brutalized and raised with low goals and lower expectations. They must be removed from the ghettos to temporary institutions where they can be inculcated with the values they will have to possess to become productive members of society. And middle-class blacks should willingly shoulder the burden of voluntarily staffing these institutions on one year leaves of absence from their jobs.

The time has come for new and different approaches; we have to be willing to try them.

CONCLUSION

As RISING CRIME STATISTICS and even faster rising national concern in-dicate, we are losing the War on Crime. The more our crime prevention strategies fail to produce the desired results the louder the clamor for more of the same policies which got us into this bewildering predicament in the first place.

If history is indeed the most accurate predictor of the future then it seems we are destined to continue wasting valuable time, energy, and resources attempting to fit the square pegs of poverty-generated crime into the round holes of strictly punishment-based solutions. It should by now be obvious to anyone that poverty and racism can breed criminals much faster than society can build prisons to house them.

As Kurt Schmoke, the mayor of Baltimore, stated, on the issue of drug decriminalization, "What I'm proposing *may* not work; but what we're presently doing *cannot* work." Congress passes petty, spiteful, and useless measures, such as the removal of weights from prison recreation yards, in an effort to convince the public that it is doing something meaningful about crime, only to have convicts resort to using stacks of magazines wrapped with strips of bed sheets or mop buckets filled with water to accomplish the same end. Evidently some in this country feel they can up the punishment ante until criminals cry uncle, but they are mistaken. Prisoners will either adjust to the new realities or riot.

The logic, however, behind cancelling Pell Grant funds for convict education, in light of the fact additional education has been proved to reduce recidivism, escapes me completely. It's as if the stratification of America has not only produced two separate and distinct classes but two languages also. "What we have here is a failure to communicate." Disgust from the haves is met with mistrust from the have-nots. Those who control the resources which are direly needed to cause meaningful change in the condition of the underclass are so far removed from that underclass and their everyday problems, the meager solutions they offer usually miss the mark entirely. Just enough funds are carelessly dumped into the abyss of neglect to insure that the degrading conditions of those stuck on the bottom rung of the economic ladder will be perpetuated.

The powerless underclass, on the other hand, has all too often completely given up any attempts to rise above their condition. Far too many have existed in abject poverty for so long they have downwardly adjusted their expectations to match their realities. It doesn't take a government-backed program to mount neighborhood cleanup efforts, or to take an active interest in their children's education.

Many in the underclass know how to respond to their degraded condition with only anger and hate. Ministers of a quasi-Muslim religion exploit these feelings to draw rancorous crowds to college campuses to listen to their hate-filled message. In one sense, this is good—America needs to look into the eyes and hear the words of the bestial demagogues racism has created.

If hatred of Jews or anyone else would ameliorate the condition of my race, improve it one small bit, I would be first in line with hate of the most vitriolic variety. But how, in the name of any God anyone chooses to worship, can hatred directed at a race or group of people possibly help us? We must reserve our enmity for the correct target: the racist institutions which keep us in an oppressed condition.

Even against the right targets our weapons must be a forceful, constant, and logical pressure applied in a no-nonsense manner; otherwise we are at risk of allowing the system which has attempted to obliterate us instead to turn us into monsters similar to those we have struggled so valiantly against. If that happens we lose even as we win.

These orgies of animosity currently being staged under the banner of racial solidarity do little more than provide emotional release for pent-up frustrations. They are frustrations we sorely need to harness, convert into useful energy, and properly redirect. These propagators of venom and nonsense, who take a grain of truth and attempt to construct a spurious argument to support their twisted views, don't offer constructive methods to actually solve the problems affecting black Americans, and probably do damage by sidetracking us from productive efforts.

Some of our youths of the underclass are lost to us; nothing we can do at this point will redeem them. They have crossed their own personal Rubicon in terms of their commitment to lives of violent crime. Only time may eventually save them from themselves. For these individuals, incarceration until they no longer pose a threat to society is the only answer. We must not waste our efforts on lost causes. But we must demand that the system do everything within its power to prevent *another* generation from being lost to the negative influences of bigotry and neglect.

Since it is evident that a high percentage of the youth raised in our nation's ghettos will eventually turn to a life of crime, it only takes common sense to devise intervention programs which will prevent this from occurring. Why do we have to wait until they mature into young, hate-filled adults, only too willing to take revenge on society with the knife, gun, and Louisville Slugger before we address their problems?

Our much cherished tradition of insuring the liberties of the individual against the state has prevented us from designing the regimented but loving Children's Camps which are vitally necessary to save another generation from the debilitating influences of our nation's ghettos. The whole concept of protecting the liberties of those who have no future other than prison is a cruel perversion of the intent of our Bill of Rights. What good is liberty to those mired in ignorance, poverty, and crime when it only allows them the freedom to die an early death?

To break the cycle of despair which has made prisoners of the underclass, even while they remain supposedly free, we have to provide safe and sane environments where we can deliver to children the messages and values they will need to be successful in society at large. Since social programs already pay for everything in these children's lives at present, providing these services in a setting where we can better control the outcome of our efforts should be a matter of simple responsibility.

Any costs incurred by such efforts, which are the only means of actually reducing crime, have to be viewed as the penalty America must pay for allowing years of unrelenting, unrepentant, and untrammeled racism foster. Hate indeed has its wages.

Those who would rather continue to pay that price in the form of additional expenses for more prisons and the costs of shattered lives of both the victims and perpetrators of crimes, rather than give up their habit of bigotry, must be completely ignored. They would bankrupt the country rather than give up their outdated modes of thinking. Better that America pay up now to correct the social conditions created by racism rather than continue to endure the resulting crime and social disorder that racism will produce for untold generations to come. Peace, be still.